Promises, Promises

Promises, Promises

Contracts in Russia and other
Post-Communist Economies

Paul H. Rubin

Professor of Economics, Emory University, USA

THE SHAFTESBURY PAPERS, 11
SERIES EDITOR: CHARLES K. ROWLEY

Edward Elgar
Cheltenham, UK • Northampton, MA, USA

Published by
Edward Elgar Publishing Limited
8 Lansdown Place
Cheltenham
Glos GL50 2HU
UK

Edward Elgar Publishing, Inc.
6 Market Street
Northampton
Massachusetts 01060
USA

A catalogue record for this book
is available from the British Library

Library of Congress Cataloguing in Publication Data
Rubin, Paul H.
    Promies, promises : contracts in Russia and other post-communist
economies / Paul H. Rubin.
        — (The Shaftesbury papers : 11)
    Includes bibliographical references and index.
    1. Contracts—Russia (Federation)   2. Contracts—Europe, Eastern.
I. Title.   II. Series.
KLB858.R83   1998
346.4702—dc21   97–38256
                                                                CIP

ISBN 1 85898 558 7

Typeset by Manton Typesetters, 5–7 Eastfield Road, Louth, Lincolnshire LN11 7AJ, UK.
Printed and bound in Great Britain by Biddles Ltd, Guildford and King's Lynn

Contents

Acknowledgements

IRIS (Institutional Reform and the Informal Sector), at the University of Maryland initially contributed to this research.

I presented earlier versions of parts of this work at Emory, George Mason, Harvard and Lund Universities, at a World Bank seminar in the Czech Republic, at the Winter 1994 American Economics Association Meetings, and at a seminar at the Political Economy Research Center in Montana.

I would like to thank Peter Aranson, Martin Bailey, George Benston, Harold Berman, Jurgen Backhaus, Michael Block, Chris Clague, John Lott, Todd Merolla, Fred McChesney and Fred Pryor and especially Jean Tesche for helpful comments. In addition, assistance in various forms, including discussions of Eastern Europe and information about sources of information, was received from Dan Drachtman, Cheryl Gray, Heidi Kroll, Russell Pittman, Nancy Roth Remington and Jan Svenjar. In Europe I had useful discussions with Ronald Dwight, Allan Farber, Peter Fath, Randall Filer, Attila Harmathy, Zoltan Jakab, Laszlo Keckes, Vladimir Laptev, Katherine Martin, Ryszard Markiewicz, Carol Patterson, Andrew Pike, Vladimir Prokop, Roman Rewald, William Sievers, Tomasz Stawecki, Lubos Tichy, Boris Topornin, Tibor Varady, Karl Viehe, Alena Zemplinerova and John Zimmerman. None of these people necessarily agrees with the implications of this work, and of course none is responsible for any errors.

Related papers have previously been published: 'Private Mechanisms for the Creation of Efficient Institutions for Market Economies', in Laszlo Somogyi, (ed.), *The Political Economy of the Transition Process in Eastern Europe*, Edward Elgar, 1993; 'Growing a Legal System in the Post-Communist Economies', *Cornell International Law Journal*, Winter, 1994, 1–47; 'Growing a Post-Communist Legal System', in Terry Anderson and P.J. Hill (eds), *The Privatization Process: A Worldwide Perspective*, Rowman & Littlefield, 1996, 57–80.

I would also like to thank Charles Rowley and the Locke Institute for editorial suggestions.

1. Introduction

An integral part of 'Civil Society' is the 'Rule of Law', by which I mean an objective, impersonal method of establishing and protecting property rights and enforcing agreements. Creation of a rule of law, like the creation of any other part of the infrastructure needed for economic growth, is an investment. As with any other investment, agents will create a rule of law only if discount rates are low enough for the investment to pay. If agents discount the future at too high a rate, investment will not be profitable. Uncertainty about the future can increase the discount rate to the point where otherwise profitable investments will not be worthwhile.

While Poland, the Czech Republic and perhaps Hungary and other formerly communist countries have solved this problem, there is some doubt about Russia. The great danger facing Russia today is that there is so much uncertainty that few agents will undertake investments that would otherwise be profitable and that would promote economic growth. This problem may be pervasive in the economy, and may serve to hamper investments of all sorts.

Weingast (1995) presents a theory of the institutional stability needed to maintain markets. He argues that if enough citizens are fearful of government institutions, then it is possible to devise what he calls a 'market-preserving federalist system'. Without such a system, it is difficult to give government the proper amount of power. Rather government tends to accrue too much power to allow a market to function. While citizens in Russia probably have a proper and well-earned scepticism of government, the institutions needed for a federalist system are clearly lacking. In Weingast's view, this means that government cannot be relied upon to create and maintain proper market-preserving institutions. Thus Weingast's theory offers an explanation for the observed uncertainty and consequent high discount rates in Russia. This theory would imply that many socially valuable market-preserving institutions would be lacking in Russia.

In this work, I consider only one manifestation of this problem: the effect on contractual performance. Efficient enforcement of contracts requires investment by several types of agent. The parties to putative contracts must themselves be willing to invest in reputations and in other types of capital for contracts to work. In addition, government agents must be willing to undertake certain investments to enforce contracts. These investments are of three sorts. First, government must be willing to create efficient contract law, either through a common law process or through a statutory (code) system. Second, it must be willing to use this law actually to enforce contracts. This requires the establishment of a well-functioning court system. Finally, government agents must be willing to honour those contracts and agreements that they themselves enter into.

These conditions seem to be met, at least to some extent, in some of the post-communist economies, but not in all. Again Russia seems to be the case where the conditions are least satisfied. Indeed in the situation of Russia today there is sufficient uncertainty so that even the 'mafia', organized criminal gangs, may find discount rates too high to make investment in contractual enforcement worthwhile.

This monograph is a normative application of law and economics scholarship to the problem of securing an efficient (wealth maximizing) method of enforcing agreements and thus facilitating exchange in the post-communist countries.[1] I do not set forth the detailed tenets of explicit law. Rather I discuss the policies that states can adopt that will allow the law to evolve efficiently. In this scheme, no one need decide *ex ante* what the outcome of the process will be.

THE PROBLEM ADDRESSED

While it is generally agreed that all law needs improvement in post-communist economies, most writing by economists on the 'transition' has dealt with property law. The key issue addressed has been privatization. A major controversy in this literature has been the optimal speed of adjustment: should there be a 'big bang' (rapid immediate privatization) or should the transition proceed at a more modest pace? Relatively little scholarly attention from economists has been devoted to other branches of law.[2]

In this work I deal with the law governing exchange and transactions. These issues are important. For example, Douglass North (1991, 481) indicates that, 'how agreements are enforced is the single most important determinant of economic performance'. North discusses the value of both formal (legal) enforcement of agreements and also the sort of informal mechanisms discussed below.

By 'exchange and transactions', I mean more than what is considered in the legal literature as contract. I include the law dealing with all voluntary agreements. Although this work focuses on contracts for exchange of goods, the principles developed apply more broadly. Securities law, the law of corporate governance, the law of secured property, labour law and bankruptcy are all areas where parties form voluntary agreements and where the arguments advanced here are relevant. Contemporary Western legal systems have erred by interfering excessively with freedom of contract in misguided and largely unsuccessful efforts to generate increased equality. For legal systems of newer economies attempting to grow quickly, it is especially desirable not to commit similar errors.

Contract law is easier to reform than is property law because signing a contract is *ex ante* a positive sum, cooperative game. While negotiating a contract, the interests of the parties are symmetric and both seek the most efficient contract. If a contract is signed in good faith (that is, if neither party plans *ex ante* to break the contract), then parties also have identical *ex ante* interests in methods of settling disputes *ex post*, when the contract has been broken. When the contract is signed, both parties want the most efficient dispute resolution mechanism because this will maximize the *ex ante* surplus to be divided between them. Of course, there may be disputes about the division of the surplus – the price term. Moreover, if there is a breach, then interests diverge. Each party wants the other to bear the costs of the breach. But initially there is agreement on contractual terms.[3]

This commonality of interest is generally much weaker, or even entirely lacking, in other bodies of law. In creating property rights in the post-communist economies, the interests of most players diverge initially. Managers, workers and ordinary citizens all want for themselves ownership rights in existing businesses and, with respect to these rights, the issue of distribution is purely competitive. Therefore, even though there might be substantial gains from creation of property rights, it is difficult to form a coalition in favour of any one scheme. (For a discussion of these difficulties, see Boycko *et al.* (1994).) Moreover, as we see in Chapter 6, in Russia, even after apparent agreement has been reached on allocation of property rights, some actors unilaterally can alter the distribution, creating additional uncertainty.

In accident law the parties are generally strangers before the accident occurs, and so there is no room for *ex ante* agreement. Once the accident occurs, of course, interests are purely in conflict: each party wants the other to bear the costs.

Those interested in law reform can use this symmetry of interests in contract to encourage efficient exchange and to design efficient contract law. There are three related points, the elaboration of which forms the heart of this work. First, in many cases law itself will not be needed. There are many mechanisms available that private parties can use to make agreements self-enforcing. Second, the law can facilitate the use of these mechanisms. For example, the law can agree to enforce arbitration clauses in contracts if parties insert such clauses.[4] This will result in settlement of many disputes without relying on the scarce resources available to the judicial system. Finally, public law can adopt the rules developed privately by arbitrators and others. This will speed up the process of development of the legal system and will ultimately lead to a more efficient system.

Obviously, a system of contract enforcement is more valuable if property rights are clearly defined. Better defined rights facilitate exchange, and the value of exchange increases with the value of the rights. Nonetheless, in designing efficient contract law, it is *not* true that 'everything depends on everything else'. Even with the existing level of property rights definitions, large amounts of exchange take place in the post-communist economies. Individuals are not self-sufficient. More efficient contract law can facilitate this existing exchange and encourage additional transactions, even under current circumstances. As privatization proceeds, more and more transactions will come under the scope of contract principles. If correct mechanisms can be adopted to allow contract law to develop efficiently, then the law can evolve with the economy. At each step in the process, the law can be useful and valuable, and if the law is more efficient it will be more valuable.

As one Russian broker told the *New York Times* (Uchitelle, 1992): 'Russian businessmen have gone ahead of the law, but goods have to move'. This same story indicates that: 'The free market, in effect, is not waiting for a legal system. Deals march on, although the contracts that are bringing the new ventures to life might be difficult to enforce'. If contracts were easier to enforce, deals would march on faster and more deals would be done.

The process described here can proceed independently of the rate of privatization. If the process is rapid, then there will be more transactions to be covered by contract than if the process is slow. However, in either case the principles identified here are applicable. Indeed there are even incentives for dictatorships to design efficient principles for private exchange, so that even if democracy should not survive in some countries the principles discussed here might be relevant for policy-makers. Even communist countries had provided limited incentives for efficient contracting (Kroll 1987).

PLAN OF THE WORK

One alternative to my proposal for gradual evolution of the law is a method of transforming contract law analogous to the 'big bang'. Some have suggested that the post-communist economies should adopt whole-sale the commercial code of an existing market economy. Others may attempt to draft such a body of law *de novo*. In Chapter 2, I discuss these proposals and indicate why I do not believe they would be feasi-ble. I indicate that, even if such a proposal were adopted, a process such as the one I describe would be needed to adapt the law efficiently to the countries in transition. I also discuss the major alternative method of legal change, the adoption by legislatures of civil codes. While the countries of interest are generally civil code countries, there are some advantages to a common law process. One option is a use of a common law process until the laws and the underlying political systems have reached some level of equilibrium. If this option is chosen, there are advantages to a private, as opposed to a public, common law process.

In Chapter 3, I discuss the economics of contract law. An important function of this law is to reduce *ex post* opportunism. I provide some evidence that opportunistic behaviour is occurring in the post-commu-nist economies. There are private mechanisms available to individuals to avoid opportunism. These mechanisms are analysed in Chapter 4. In Chapter 5, I discuss in more detail the current legal situations in the Czech Republic, Hungary and Poland. In these three countries, while there are flaws and law is not complete, nonetheless there is a sound body of commercial law in place.

Chapter 6, the longest in the book, discusses Russia. In Russia, in contrast to the other countries, the law is much weaker and much more reform is needed. I provide numerous examples of legal failures. How-ever, many of the problems seem to stem in part from *insufficient* central government power, so that differing levels of government cannot commit to honour agreements.[5] This in turn seems to derive from uncertainty and the associated high discount rates. I also discuss some mechanisms in place that may serve to enforce agreements, and the possibility of organized crime serving an enforcement function. I conclude that it is at this time impossible to tell if Russia will undertake a successful development, although there are reasons for fearing that it will not.

Chapter 7 outlines and analyses government policies that facilitate efficient transactional rules. There are things that governments should do to facilitate exchange. There are also things that governments should refrain from doing that hinder exchange. Both types of policy are discussed.

Chapter 8 relates the informal mechanisms discussed earlier to the process of evolution of efficient rules. It is shown that a combination of formal and informal mechanisms may be the fastest way to achieve efficient rules. For example, drafters of legal codes can incorporate lessons learned about efficient law from the informal mechanisms into their code revisions.

Chapter 9 summarizes the practical implications of the work. There are implications for the behaviour of government, arbitrators, private trade associations, private attorneys and businesses.

Because changes in Russia and in Eastern Europe are continuing, it is important to note the timeliness of this work. I have attempted to make the work up to date to December 1995. There have just been elections in Russia. The results of these elections – significant gains in power for the communists and nationalists – do not seem likely to lead to significant improvements in the behaviour of the country with respect to the matters discussed here.

2. Alternative Methods of Legal Change

In this chapter, I discuss the major alternatives to a common law, evolutionary process for legal change.

A 'BIG BANG' FOR CONTRACT LAW?

There are equivalents in contract law to the 'big bang' proposals for rapid privatization of property. One is the suggestion made by several authorities that the post-communist economies adopt entirely the civil code of some capitalist economy such as Finland or the Netherlands (for example, Leijonhufvud 1993).

Such a code would be difficult to interpret for an economy with no tradition of markets. Indeed even translating the terms from Finnish or Dutch into Russian or Polish would be difficult. The terms are defined only by their use in a market economy and in actual existing transactions and decisions. Leoni (1961) discusses the difficulty of translating legal terms from one language to another because words are rooted in institutions that may be lacking in the second culture. Leoni's discussion is in the context of translating between languages used in relatively free economies; the problems would be exacerbated in trying to translate terms used in market economies to languages spoken in societies that have not had markets and the corresponding institutions for many years. Murrell (1991) makes a similar point by suggesting that a legal code has embedded in it large amounts of practical knowledge, so that a transfer would not be feasible.[6]

Leoni also discusses the problems arising from the fact that it may seem possible to translate words that have different meanings in different legal cultures. We may identify examples of this problem. The Russian 'Arbitration Court' is the general court with business jurisdiction; the term 'arbitration' is not the same as arbitration in English. 'Commercial bank', 'leaseholding property' and 'stockholding' are all used differently in Russian law than in other jurisdictions (Tourevski and Morgan 1993). In Russia, bonds are short-term obligations and bills long term, the opposite of the Western usage, and it requires three sentences to define 'cash flow' (Kranz and Miller 1994). Other such inconsistencies would undoubtedly be found, but if they were found after the adoption of a code substantial problems could be created.

It takes three years for an American college graduate (who has grown up in a market economy) to learn in law school the meaning of US law, and longer until this knowledge is useful in a practical sense. Businessmen must then rely on discussions with trained attorneys in order for the law to affect their behaviour. To expect to circumvent this process simply by adopting an existing code is not realistic.

Similarly, it would not be feasible for authorities to generate an entire body of contract law *de novo*. Difficulties are not a result of incorrect drafting by the legislature, and could not be corrected by better craftsmanship. A body of law such as contract law is in some sense organically grown over a long period of time. It has numerous components that must interact with each other and with other large, complex bodies of law (securities law, corporate law and labour law, to name but a few). As Hayek (1973, 65) says: 'The parts of a legal system are not so much adjusted to each other according to a comprehensive overall view, as gradually adapted to each other by the successive application of general principles to particular problems'. Laws must also be adapted to existing institutions in an economy.

Schmid (1992) points out that contract law may adopt one set of risk-sharing doctrines in a world where market insurance is freely available, but that these institutions may not be desirable if such insurance markets are lacking. For anyone or any group to be able to craft such a body of law is as unlikely as for a single decision-maker to be able to design a complex economy *de novo*. It was of course the impossibility of this latter task (the socialist calculation problem) that caused the current situation in the former Soviet Empire.

When a complex statute (such as the Americans with Disabilities Act, 1990) is adopted in the USA, it commonly takes some years of litigation before its meaning is fully clear. While some blame this on poor drafting by the legislature, it is also true that no one *ex ante* can predict fully the meaning of such a major legal change and its relationship with other law. If American law-makers with large staffs of experienced professional lawyers and input from many others cannot fully predict the implications of only one statute, how could we expect

Russian or Polish law-makers lacking experience in a private law environment to be able to craft an entire code?

All the countries here under consideration have some sort of pre-existing contract law. Therefore the choice is not between starting *de novo* or adopting a body of law. Rather the choice is between modifying an existing body of law or adopting some other body of law. However, even if some other country's law were to be adopted, it would require modification to tailor the law to local conditions (where these conditions include the lack of market institutions for many years). Thus in either case, the issue is the most efficient method of modifying some currently maladapted law. The proposals in this work are useful for adapting a body of law to relevant local circumstances, whatever its original source.

COMMON LAW OR CIVIL CODE?

The two major methods of deriving the law governing private relations (property, contracts, tort) are common law and civil codes. Codes are passed by legislatures; common law is judge-made law. Britain and its former colonies (including the USA[7]) use common law; most of the rest of the world, including the post-communist economies (now and before communism), use legislative codes. Nonetheless, I argue here for at least a temporary use of common law principles in these countries.

General arguments in favour of common law in all circumstances have been proposed by Hayek (1973), Posner (1992), Rubin (1977) and Scully (1992). Here I make the more limited argument that, for the conditions in which the post-communist countries now find themselves, a reliance for a time on common law-like processes would be useful. This reliance would not preclude the use of codes, but would be a useful supplement. Indeed a private common law-like process would be even better.

The process of code-drafting generally requires the time of skilled lawyers (often, in advanced countries, academic lawyers) and of legislatures. Generally a commission of attorneys will draft a proposed code that will be submitted to the legislature. The legislature will then request comments from interested and politically relevant parties. This process may go through several iterations. In contrast, common law decisions are by-products of the judicial dispute resolution process.

The argument here is that as a factual matter the relative price of legislators and skilled lawyers is higher in the post-communist countries than elsewhere. Thus whatever the optimal balance between common law and code in more settled countries, the optimal mix is more towards a common law process in the newer economies.

Consider first lawyers. In order to draft a code, what is needed is a lawyer with knowledge of local conditions and laws, but also with knowledge of Western capitalist law. Obviously, law schools in communist regimes did not specialize in training such attorneys, and there are relatively few of them. Their scarcity means that today such attorneys have a high opportunity cost because there is a private market for their services.[8] Code-drafting is not a highly paid occupation; it is commonly performed as part of academic responsibility. Governments in all the countries studied are not likely to pay high wages to attorneys to draft such codes. This does not mean that private attorneys would refuse if asked to serve on code-drafting commissions. Rather they would likely take longer to provide a draft than would otherwise occur. Thus the first input into code-drafting, attorneys' time, seems scarcer in the post-communist economies than would be true at an equilibrium.

Legislator time is also scarce. The relevant countries are in the process of creating new economic, political and social orders. For such efforts, new laws and legislation are necessary. For example, privatization is itself a major change requiring substantial legislative input. In Russia the legislature has been busy with major political decisions, such as determining the role of the various geographic and ethnic components of the country in the new state. Again this means that if a code is proposed to a legislature by a commission, the legislature is likely to take a longer time in responding than otherwise. Legal changes in codes are not high on the political agenda.

Boris Topornin (1993), Director of the Institute of State and Law of the Russian Academy of Sciences, addressed this issue. He indicated that the 'first generation' of Russian laws, adopted in December 1990, were 'insufficiently clear' and 'insufficiently systematic'. Topornin indicated that current (1993) Russian law was inadequate, and that during the transition it would be necessary to change the law rapidly. However, the first generation of laws governed in Russia for some years. The legislature took a long time to pass a 'second generation'. Some of these laws have now been passed but, as outlined below, substantial problems remain and new drafts are needed. Again there have been delays in passing these newer laws. Although Topornin indicates that

Russian law is fundamentally a code system, he also agrees that it might be possible to, 'use the experience of the common law'.

In this context, a major benefit of a common law process is that decisions and legal change occur as a by-product of dispute resolution. Whenever a dispute is settled by an appellate court, then new law is made (if there is a written opinion). Since courts naturally settle disputes, generation of common law is relatively cheap. The only cost is the cost of the judges' time in writing an opinion, as opposed to merely providing a decision. In the post-communist countries, this cost might be higher because judges lack experience.

The trade-off between code and common law systems is in terms of the rate of adaptation of the law to changing conditions. Ideally a code can achieve the optimum set of laws when it is first adopted. In contrast, the common law will never reach optimality. However, as soon as a code is passed it begins to become obsolete, and its maladaptation increases until a new code is adopted. The common law, on the other hand, is always somewhat maladapted, but its lack of adaptation is limited because it is continually changing. In deciding which form of law is most desirable, a country must balance these two types of cost. Since in countries in legal disarray (such as the new economies), adoption of new codes takes relatively longer than in countries in equilibrium, the balance predictably shifts relatively more towards a common law solution.

Moreover, while a shift to a common law-like process would be a change for legal systems that are not accustomed to such a process, the change need not be permanent. Legislatures could announce that rulings by appellate courts would have the force of law until a new codification of the relevant body of law could be passed. These decisions could then be an input into the codification process, but only one input. Such a system would allow some of the benefits of a common law process without eliminating the legal traditions of the relevant countries.

PRIVATE LAW OR PUBLIC LAW?

An even simpler reform would be to rely on a private common law system. Indeed it might be possible to establish such a system with minimal state intervention. The state would need to agree to enforce decisions reached by arbitrators. If it were well known that the state would enforce such decisions, actual enforcement would seldom be required. If such enforcement were available, arbitrators (or associations of arbitrators) themselves could announce that they planned to establish a common law-like system and follow precedent in decision-making.

Once the system of precedents became established, then parties would generally not rely on the arbitrators. Just as most disputes settle out of court, so would we expect most disputes under an arbitration system with a body of common law precedents to settle without a formal hearing. The arbitration association could charge a fee for being named in an agreement as the final arbitrator of potential disputes and refuse to arbitrate any dispute between parties who had not named it. In this way the arbitration association could be compensated for the public good provided when decisions were written (Benson 1990).

Later I discuss some benefits of arbitration. However, many benefits arise because the courts in the relevant countries are themselves in some disarray. In general, a major problem is the lack of skilled personnel – lawyers and judges – for dealing with commercial dispute resolution and contract enforcement. This is due to lack of experience with appropriate law and institutions. While the main principles of contract law in many of the relevant countries are consistent with a market economy, the principles have never been applied directly to contracts between enterprises in free markets. Current judges do not have the required experience, and most countries have not trained many such judges. Moreover, business operators and even lawyers are not familiar with contracts because of the nature of the functioning of the communist system. Since parties will be able to choose arbitrators, there will be selection of those most able to solve the problems associated with particular contracts, whether they be local or Western lawyers, experienced businessmen or professional arbitrators.

As of 1995, Russian courts lack sufficient power. Kornai (1992) indicates that Hungarian courts lack experience with a market economy and lack sufficient resources to adjudicate all disputes that arise in a market economy. Gray and Associates (1993), in their discussions of law in Poland, Hungary and the Czech Republic, indicate in all cases that trained judges are lacking, and that both the legal system and the population at large lack experience in a market economy. Aslund (1992) is even more pessimistic: 'To require the state to do anything means to ask the uninformed and corrupt for assistance...Therefore, the only defensible recommendation is that the role of the state should be limited to a bare minimum in the period of transition to capitalism'.

Thus there are severe difficulties in drafting and enforcing public law for contract enforcement. Moreover, the skilled resources that would be needed for this project might be better employed elsewhere. This is particularly true since it may be possible to go a fair way towards creation of such law through private mechanisms. The proposals set forth here rely much less on a formal judiciary than do proposals for more explicit public law, and may be easier to begin applying.

3. Contracts and Opportunism

The key class of problems facing potential traders in a world with no legal contract enforcement are problems of opportunism (Williamson 1985; Rubin 1990). I first discuss opportunism, and then present evidence that the problem exists in the post-communist countries.

OPPORTUNISM: THEORY

In many transactions, one party will have performed his part of the deal before the other, who will then have an incentive to cheat. One key purpose of the law of contracts is to discourage such opportunism (Muris 1981). Examples of opportunism can be so crude as simply to refuse to make an agreed-upon payment. More sophisticated forms of cheating include offering high quality goods for sale and delivering low quality (Akerlof 1970). A firm may also put a trading partner in a position where the partner is dependent on the firm for some input, and then raise the price, an action called 'hold-up'.

The general form of opportunism is appropriating the 'quasi-rents' associated with some transaction (Klein *et al.* 1978).[9] Such quasi-rents are often created by 'asset specificity', creations of valuable assets that are specialized to one transaction or trading partner. Once these specific assets are created, an opportunistic trading partner can sometimes appropriate their value.

The major cost of opportunism when it cannot effectively be prevented is neither the cost of cheating, nor even the cost of precautions taken to avoid being victimized. Rather it is the lost social value from the otherwise profitable deals that do not transpire. For example, if sellers cannot credibly promise to deliver high quality goods, then consumers will not be willing to pay a higher price for allegedly higher quality and manufacturers will therefore not produce them. Similarly, in economies with no contractual possibilities, transactors often deal with long-term associates or relatives in order to have additional assurances of contractual performance.[10] But this means that many potential transactions will not occur because otherwise suitable parties will not be in appropriate relationships and so cannot guarantee performance, even though such transactions would be value increasing.

There is another cost to the post-communist economies of lack of contractual enforcement mechanisms. As Coase (1937) pointed out, if transaction costs between firms are high, then more activity will occur within the firm and less in markets.[11] But lack of enforcement mechanisms means that firms will be relatively larger because they will internalize more functions. Many authorities have remarked on the inefficiently large size of firms in these economies, and have argued that breaking the firms into smaller parts would be desirable. However, until efficient contract enforcement mechanisms are available, the incentive for such restructuring will be reduced because managers can anticipate difficulties in using contract to achieve coordination that they now achieve by command.

In general, less formal enforcement mechanisms can work better for shorter-term transactions and for transactions involving smaller amounts of money. As the time horizon of a contract becomes longer or the amount at issue becomes larger, the value of formal enforcement increases. Thus an additional cost of lack of enforcement mechanisms is the loss of the long-term investments and the large investments deterred by the lack of enforceability (Clague *et al.* 1995). To the extent that mechanisms can be designed and adopted that reduce or eliminate opportunism, then social wealth can be greatly increased.

OPPORTUNISM: EVIDENCE

Problems of opportunism exist in the post-communist economies. During the communist period, informal small-scale trading networks based on family, ethnicity, friendship, reciprocity, long-term obligations and barter supported trade (Los 1992). Personal relations and trust are still important (Johnson and Kroll 1991). The importance of personal contacts in supporting exchange in Russia is a major theme of Tourevski and Morgan (1993), a book written to provide practical advice to Western businessmen considering investing in Russia. Such contacts are of substantial importance primarily in contexts where there are limited possibilities for more formal governance mechanisms.

Consumers complain about low quality goods. If consumers would be willing to pay higher prices for higher quality, then this indicates a market failure. Goldberg (1992) discusses quality efforts in consumer and other markets. He indicates that several new legislative proposals for increasing quality are being considered. However, none of these involve proper incentives and none create proper reputation effects. A reliance on legislation to achieve goals that markets can better provide is evidence of a carryover in thought processes from the previous economic system.

One major survey found that people in Russia have less confidence about the future and are more likely to believe that institutions are likely to change for the worse than is true of people in capitalist societies (Shiller *et al.* 1992). This would explain in part the unwillingness of owners of firms to invest in brand name capital, and is consistent with other behaviour further discussed below.

Foreign businessmen are cautious in doing business in Eastern Europe. For example, Western firms often take longer to do a job so that less investment is at risk at any point in time. They will also move more slowly in working with partners and subcontractors than would be true in a world with more legal certainty. Many foreign firms are investing in distribution networks in these countries, but not in manufacturing capacity. Part of the reason is the fear of loss of investment. Even so, firms are sometimes victimized by opportunistic Russians. Poe (1993, 158–9) describes episodes in which potential investors have spent time and money in negotiating with individuals who do not have the authority actually to agree to the contract. This problem is associated with the poor definition of property rights in Russia, so that it is difficult to determine ownership.

There is even evidence of the simplest forms of opportunism. Firms in Russia sometimes take money and provide nothing; at other times they accept goods and then do not pay. Enforcement even in these cases is apparently difficult (Buyevich and Zhukov 1992). Uchitelle (1992) indicates that buyers operating on commodity exchanges often renege. In Hungary two-thirds of the 700,000 lawsuits filed in 1991 involved debt collection (Gray and Associates 1993.) Indeed the most significant form of opportunism in the post-communist societies may be simple failure to pay debts. In Hungary, bankruptcy law can be used for debt collection, but such mechanisms are less well developed in other countries.

There is also evidence that the structure of new private firms is due in part to uncertainty about contract enforcement. Many new firms in

Russia are forming holding companies or using vertical integration in order to guarantee needed supplies. Indeed one 'consultant' indicated explicitly that this was the motivation for organizing a large firm containing many otherwise independent firms. Many new firms are associated with existing state firms, again for the purpose of obtaining guarantees of contractual performance (Johnson and Kroll 1991).

In addition to opportunism by firms, there is also a massive problem of government opportunism in Russia. Governments seem to lure investments by making particular promises, and then expropriate the quasi-rents associated with these investments by changing the rules. I discuss this issue in more detail in Chapter 6 when I discuss the problems of Russia.

4. Private Mechanisms

There are several mechanisms that parties could use to facilitate exchange where contracts will not work. Even in developed countries, explicit enforceable (and enforced) contracts are relatively unimportant for much exchange. In the USA 75 per cent of commercial disputes are settled privately through arbitration and mediation (Benson 1990, 2). However, businesses in developed economies have learned (perhaps through trial and error) methods of doing substantial amounts of business without relying on contracts and, of course, the threat of legal enforcement makes private arrangements easier. Businesses in new economies will have less experience with such techniques.

It is helpful to classify private mechanisms that can be used to make agreements credible into three classes, depending on the number of parties involved in generating the enforcement mechanism. All three are based on reputations. These mechanisms are discussed in more detail in Rubin (1993).

UNILATERAL MECHANISMS

The major class of unilateral mechanisms is investments in reputation. Advertising is one form of such investment (Klein and Leffler 1981). Firms can invest in expensive signs or logos that become worthless if the firm cheats. Law firms invest in expensive decor serving the same function.

However, while firms can privately invest in reputation creation, there are some difficulties in the Eastern countries (and in particular in Russia) in this process. Traditionally firms in these countries have valued secrecy, rather than the openness needed for reputations to work: 'Very often Soviet participants take a closed or secretive position and the attempts to hide information can reach ridiculous levels' (Tourevski and Morgan 1993, 245); 'Foreign investors need to be aggressive about getting information, because by inclination and long-standing habit, companies won't divulge it' (Kvint 1993, 79). It is not clear why firms are excessively secretive, but such behaviour can be counterproductive. One possible explanation is that in bargaining, firms have often been concerned with making sure that their partner did not make a profit or surplus, rather than with maximizing any measure of joint surplus. As discussed below, this bargaining strategy may itself be due to short time horizons caused by uncertainty. In addition, fear of organized crime or of excessive government taxation can lead to excess secrecy.

BILATERAL MECHANISMS

Bilateral mechanisms are those involving only two firms, often a buyer and a seller. Three relevant types of bilateral arrangement are: self-enforcing contracts; vertical relationships between dealers and manu-facturers; and the use of 'hostages', including collateral. It might ap-pear that contracts including private arbitration clauses would be rel-evant here, but as we see below, these fit better into the multilateral analysis.

Self-Enforcing Agreements

The most important type of bilateral mechanism is the creation of what has been called a 'self-enforcing agreement' (Telser 1980). This is an agreement between two firms that contains no external enforcement provisions. The agreement operates as long as it is in the interest of both firms to maintain it. For each firm, the value of the agreement is the value of the expected future business from maintaining the relation-ship. If a firm cheats, then it gains in the short run but loses the value of the future business. If discount rates are high in Russia because of uncertainty about the future, then such agreements would be less likely to work because the present value of the future business would be reduced.

Uchitelle (1992) indicates that exactly this sort of contract is now occurring in Russia: '...two concepts – mutual benefit and trust – have come to play a major role in these early days of Russian capitalism. What these concepts come down to is this: If both parties to an agreement are benefiting from the deal, presumably they will not break the contract'.

Nonetheless, there seems to be a tradition in Russia of hard bargain-ing: 'Soviet negotiators see business deals as fixed and finite entities.

Only when ensuring that they end up with more and the negotiating partners end up with less do they feel the negotiations are successful' (Tourevski and Morgan 1993, 243); 'One of the chief criteria for evaluating how foreign trade officials do their job is the discount they generate during negotiations, which is supposed to show how persistent and uncompromising they are as businessmen' (Tourevski and Morgan 1993, 243). As long as this sort of bargaining occurs, it will be difficult to establish self-enforcing agreements.

Burandt (1992) discusses the formation of a joint venture for advertising between a Russian organization and the American advertising agency, Young and Rubicam. Young and Rubicam would price its services and pay the media 'fairly' because the goal was to, 'establish ourselves as a reputable and leading company in this business for the long haul'. On the other hand: 'It wasn't atypical in the Soviet Union for organizations to overcharge customers and underpay suppliers'. In other words, Burandt is arguing for prices that would make agreements self-enforcing, and such prices seem to be less common in Russia.

Vertical Controls

An interesting class of bilateral transactions is between manufacturers and retailers of the product. There are various policies that manufacturers with brand name capital might want retailers to carry out. Some are: demonstrating and advertising the product; certification of quality; maintaining freshness; promoting the product to marginal consumers; maintenance of complete inventories; and refraining from 'switching' customers to alternative product lines when consumers respond to manufacturers' advertisements.

There are numerous mechanisms that can achieve these goals. These include: establishment of maximum or minimum prices for the sale of goods (resale price maintenance); territorial restrictions (including exclusive territories); requirements that dealers carry only the brand of the manufacturer (exclusive dealing); and requirements of certain methods of retailing (such as shelf space requirements). Manufacturers may also integrate directly into retailing or may establish franchises for selling their product. It is not my purpose here to discuss the business reasons for these restrictions; such discussions are available elsewhere (Rubin 1990, Chapter 6). These restrictions can be carried out as self-enforcing agreements, with the threat of termination as the only sanction. There is no need for state enforcement of these types of arrangement. However, state hostility (as, for example, through much American antitrust law) can make such agreements non-viable.

Franchising might be particularly useful in the former communist economies. There are many excessively large and excessively centralized enterprises. Splitting some of these entities into separate firms linked through franchise contracts could be a useful way of decentralizing without losing the benefits (if any) of a common brand name. The relationships between components of many large Russian enterprises are already similar to relationships between franchisors and franchisees (Poe 1993). Poland is successfully developing a franchise system, although most of the franchisors are American and European firms (Simpson 1995). One additional important benefit of this method of business development is the training provided by the franchisors.

Hostages

One way for a firm to commit to not cheating is to offer a hostage to its trading partner. A simple hostage is collateral: a cash deposit that will be lost if the firm cheats. Such a hostage requires some outside enforcement, but not by the state. For example, the firms could jointly hire an attorney who would be empowered to decide if cheating had occurred and to award the payment to the victim. Of course, there is a problem in trusting the attorney not to expropriate the hostage. However, firms might exist whose sole value is their reputation capital for enforcing such agreements and who therefore would not have an incentive to cheat in this way as long as their reputations were worth more than any one hostage. Law firms or investment banking firms might be able to perform this function. International firms might be particularly well suited for this role because they have established valuable reputations.

A more natural method is the creation of bilateral hostages. If firm A is dependent on firm B for some input, then firm A would have an incentive to put firm B in a position of being dependent on firm A as well. Moreover, firm B would have an incentive to be put in this position in order to be able to guarantee not to cheat. For example, firms making cardboard boxes commonly trade components with each other across geographic areas, and in this case neither firm can hold up the other without also putting itself at risk.

MULTILATERAL MECHANISMS

These are the most interesting class of adaptations, and the least well studied. A well-defined multilateral arrangement involving a group of member firms can enforce honest dealing both between members of the group and between members and outsiders. The Law Merchant (the medieval body of commercial law) was exactly this sort of multilateral private legal system that enforced honesty by threats of reputation loss (see for example, Berman 1983, Benson 1990 and Milgrom *et al.* 1990). The Law Merchant was then adopted into English common law. Similar institutions survive today in advanced countries. The Better Business Bureau, for example, is a reputation-guaranteeing device with properties similar to those of the Law Merchant. Many trade associations have codes of ethics with many of the properties of the Law Merchant (Hill 1976).

Private contracts requiring arbitration of disputes require similar enforcement mechanisms. Much international commercial law is based on arbitration, with loss of reputation as the major sanction for breach (Benson 1992). I begin with an analysis of private arbitration that demonstrates the need for multilateral enforcement.

Arbitration

The parties to a contract can specify in the contract that, in the event of a dispute, they will settle the issue through arbitration. There will be several benefits to parties from the use of arbitration for dispute settlement.

In a world where judges may not have much experience with business disputes and where legal precedents may be weak, it should be possible to choose arbitrators who will be more likely to reach efficient decisions. Arbitrators will be paid only if hired, and so will have an incentive to reach correct decisions because this will lead to future business. If there are competing 'court' systems, or competing groups of arbitrators, the parties can select the one they desire. Parties to contracts written in good faith will not expect to breach at the time of drafting the agreement. Therefore, *ex ante* the parties will desire to select that forum for dispute resolution in which they expect to obtain the most efficient results, so that *ex ante* competition among arbitrators will favour those with a reputation for providing the most efficient (wealth maximizing) decisions. Moreover, parties can specify the amount to be paid to arbitrators. This means that arbitrators in more important (costly) disputes can be paid more, so that parties will have access to the quality of arbitrator appropriate to the value of the case.

Parties can also choose the body of law or rules that will govern in the event of a dispute. If the formal law in place is inefficient or vague, the parties can indicate that they will have their dispute governed by a different body of law, or by the rules of the arbitration association. This allows more flexibility in choice of law and means that it is more likely that an efficient law will govern. If it turns out that one body of law is generally chosen by parties, then this will be evidence that this law might be the most efficient to be used as public law. Arbitrators can sometimes use industry custom as a method of determining liability. Indeed much common law and most commercial law are ultimately based on custom.

However, in the post-communist societies custom is likely to be less useful as a basis for law than has traditionally been true. Those who write of custom as a basis for law have in mind a situation in which trade is already occurring and a law-maker begins to use the existing customs as a basis for law (Cooter 1994); this is, for example, the approximate way in which the Law Merchant was incorporated into the common law. However, in the post-communist economies, existing custom has evolved largely in circumstances in which trade was illegal and it was necessary to hide or disguise the terms, and even existence, of exchange. Thus existing customs may be less well suited to adoption into formal law than has traditionally been true.

Indeed those who were entrepreneurs under communism may be true criminals today, and existing customs may be more suited to criminal enterprise than to normal business (Kvint 1993, 196–200; Tourevski and Morgan 1993, 210–21). As Handelman (1995, p. 49) says: 'With no clearly defined boundaries between legal and illegal economic behavior, the shrewdest criminal bosses were hard to distinguish from entrepreneurs'. Kranz (1995a) also indicates that, 'the boundary between legality and illegality has never been as blurry'. Thus whether existing customs are efficient or not depends on whether the skill of current businessmen was in engaging in trade and (at that time illegal) market transactions, or in engaging in socially unproductive or counterproductive activities. Moreover, the custom of excess secrecy, mentioned earlier, would be counterproductive in a market economy. Nonetheless, customs developed since the time of liberation onwards should be useful.

There is a limit to purely private arbitration. That limit is that the party which loses in a dispute has an incentive to ignore the decision. In countries with an established body of contract law, the solution is that the courts will often enforce the decree of the arbitrator. In a society where there is no court enforcement of such decrees, the only remedy is a reputation remedy. In small societies where reputation is common knowledge among all parties, then simple publicizing of cheating may work. However, in larger societies, where there are many trading partners, it may be necessary to devise more complex devices for private enforcement of arbitration decrees. This is the topic of the next section.

Multilateral Enforcement Devices

Consider a trade association with the following policies:

1. The association collects dues from all members. These dues are used to subsidize part of the costs of arbitration proceedings in which disputes among members, and between members and customers or suppliers are resolved. Disputants also pay part of the costs.
2. Information is made available to all potential customers and suppliers regarding the list of members, so that it is possible for a potential customer to ascertain at low cost if a potential seller is a member of the trade association.
3. If the decision of the arbitrator goes against a party and the party ignores the decision (for example, refuses to pay damages as ordered by the arbitrator), then the party will be expelled from the association.
4. Therefore, if a party has been expelled, then when a new potential trading partner queries the association, he will learn that the seller is not a member and will accordingly be able to avoid trading with the party, or will trade on different terms.

The structure of this mechanism corresponds to the Law Merchant mechanism. Milgrom *et al.* (1990) provide a game-theoretic analysis of this mechanism and show that the outcome is stable and will lead to efficient trading patterns.

This pattern is also followed by many trade associations that engage in self-policing (see Bernstein (1995), for a partial listing). (The ability to engage in self-regulation in the USA may have been excessively restricted by the application of antitrust laws.) The Code of Ethics and Interpretations of the Public Relations Society of America calls for an investigation of allegations of misconduct, with expulsion and publicity as potential remedies. This code includes interpretations based on actual cases, which form a 'body of law' (Hill 1976, 285). Similarly, the Code of Ethics of the National Association of Realtors has a provision for expulsion of members who do not accept the finding of review boards. This same pattern is followed by diamond 'bourses' (diamond exchange markets) such as the New York Diamond Dealers Club, and by the World Federation of Diamond Bourses (Bernstein, 1992). Better Business Bureaus – private reputation – enforcing groups in the USA – also follow this procedure, although these organizations also provide information about non-member firms. A simple mechanism would be for member firms to display on their doors or in their advertising a logo indicating that they are approved by the Better Business Bureau.

Trade associations and Better Business Bureaus illustrate the types of organization of reputation-guaranteeing associations that might be useful. Trade associations commonly include members of a given business, irrespective of geographic location. Conversely, Better Business Bureaus include businesses in a particular area, irrespective of the nature of the business. The latter type of organization is more likely to be useful to guarantee reputations of those who sell to consumers; the former, of those who sell to businesses.

LIMITS TO PRIVATE MECHANISMS

While private mechanisms can support some exchange, there are limits to the power of these mechanisms. It is useful to assume that a party will behave opportunistically whenever it pays to do so. Explicit enforceable agreements can mean that opportunism will be prohibitively expensive. A court order or an enforceable arbitration decree can remove any profit from opportunistic behaviour. Other mechanisms are less reliable. This means that the amount that can be exchanged without an enforceable agreement will be limited. The most that can be put at risk is the value of the reputation that would be lost if cheating occurs.

In Russia these problems are multiplied. As discussed below, public enforcement is weak. Unfortunately, private mechanisms are also relatively weak in Russia. Most such mechanisms rely on reputations, and in Russia most enterprises are new and lacking in developed reputations. Thus although reputation and contract are substitute methods of enforcing agreements (Klein 1992, 161), the situation in Russia (and to a lesser extent in the other post-communist economies considered here) is that neither mechanism is easily available.

Moreover, there are actual hindrances to the creation of reputations. Fear of extortion creates a positive value for secrecy. Criminals can use information about the reliability and success of firms for purposes of extortion (Black *et al.* 1995; Handelman 1995; Leitzel *et al.* 1995). Pistor (1995) indicates that parties are often unwilling to write complete contracts for this same reason. The same factors make tax collection difficult: firms are unwilling to tell tax collectors about revenues for fear that criminals will use this information for extortion. Frye (1995) indicates that firms are sometimes unwilling to use public contract enforcement mechanisms because of a fear of expropriation by the tax authorities themselves. Thus several factors conspire in the case of Russia to make the creation of reputation capital difficult.

This should not be taken to mean that private mechanisms are valueless. On the contrary, they are common, even in developed economies. However, it is important to realize their limits. Such mechanisms should be supported by formal enforcement devices whenever possible. Clague *et al.* (1996) suggest that a certain amount of trade occurs in all economies, but that developed economies are those that have established formal mechanisms for enforcing long-term agreements.

5. The Czech Republic, Hungary and Poland

It is not correct to view all of the post-communist countries as starting from the same point. Of those countries specifically considered here, the Czech Republic, Hungary and Poland are much more similar to each other than any is to Russia.

Albania, Bulgaria and Romania are probably somewhere in between, although privatization in these countries has not proceeded as far as in Russia. It is likely that the Baltic Republics (Latvia, Estonia and Lithuania) are similar to the first three countries, while the Ukraine and Belorussia may be similar to Russia. Some of the Asiatic republics (Uzbekistan, Turkmenistan, Kirghizstan and Tadjikistan) may be relatively less developed than Russia. The exact ranking is not important: what is relevant is the observation that the countries considered may provide examples for others.

Commerce can function with a relatively small body of contract law. Most terms of contracts are written privately by the parties themselves; as Benson (1990) points out, the parties actually make 'law' by writing a contract. Explicit public law serves two functions in addition to enforcing private terms. First, it fills gaps: it covers situations that the parties did not anticipate. Second, it supplies defaults: if the law provides certain terms or indicates certain results, the parties to a private agreement can save resources by not directly dealing with these issues, or paying lawyers to deal with them. However, the major part of the contract is the result of private agreement. Thus parties can engage in substantial amounts of contractually based commerce with little explicit 'law' on the books.

The civil codes of the countries in the former Soviet Union are based on pre-Soviet European civil codes and, 'many of the principles are not inconsistent with a market economy' (IMF 1991, 247). In many cases, these have been adopted from pre-communist codes. This is also true of the Czech Republic, Poland and Hungary. At the beginning of the transition, these three countries had in place a set of basic contract laws.

11-27

Poland's original contract law was a 1933 Western law. A commission was to redraft and update this code. In Hungary, transactions were governed by those parts of the civil code originally written to govern small, non-commercial private transactions. The Czech and Slovak Federal Republic (CSFR) had more of its legal system adapted to communism than most other countries, so that it had less law to build on than others. The CSFR adopted a new civil code and a new commercial code in 1991. Thus in many of the Eastern countries there were indigenous bodies of contract law, but none are fully adapted to contemporary business. Beginning with the existing body of contract law and allowing modifications as discussed below is likely to be the most efficient and most expeditious way to achieve a body of contract law suited to market conditions in the post-communist economies.

Gray and Associates (1993) provides a summary of the situation in Poland soon after the transition that seems to apply more generally:

> Although the legal structure is generally satisfactory in most areas, practice is still uncertain in all areas. The generality of the laws leaves wide discretion for administrators and courts, and there has not yet been time to build up a body of cases and practice to further define the rules of the game. Although the courts are in general honest and are used by the population, they have little experience in economic matters. Judges are not well paid, and the best lawyers have a strong incentive to go into private practice. The wide discretion and general lack of precedent and competence create tremendous legal uncertainty that is sure to hamper private sector development.

All four countries examined enforce arbitration clauses in contracts between domestic and foreign firms. However, as of 1993, only Poland would enforce arbitration agreements between domestic firms. Parties are allowed to specify whose law will govern and who will be the arbitrator in the event of a dispute. The Union of Polish Banks has established an arbitration court for disputes involving banks and their customers. The Polish economy recently performed better than any other formerly communist economy (Perlez 1993). Much of this is due to the productivity of Polish domestic firms, since the country had at that time received relatively little foreign investment. While all the countries studied have efficient rules with respect to arbitration for dealings with foreign investors, Poland has the most efficient system for contract enforcement involving domestic firms. It is interesting that Poland has the most favourable laws of all the countries studied and its economy is outperforming the others, although this observation is of course not proof.

The benefit of efficient laws is continuing. Anecdotal evidence indicates that Poland and the Czech Republic are greatly benefiting from the legal certainty, and Hungary is benefiting to a lesser extent. (Hungary's main problem seems to be a reluctance to privatize, rather than direct contractual uncertainty.) One piece of evidence is negative: the US business press, in writing about these countries, never mentions difficulties with the 'rule of law' or with the legal system. Even in describing cases where Western investments have been unsuccessful in the Czech Republic, Hungary and Poland, the discussion is in terms of business reasons for the failures, rather than contractual or legal difficulties (see, for example, Branegan 1994). As we see in the next chapter, this is totally different from the case of Russia; there, virtually every article discusses legal uncertainty and difficulties with contract enforcement. Moreover, in comparing Eastern Europe with Russia, the point is often made that legal systems are much more advanced in the former countries (see, for example, Pennar *et al.* 1994).

Poland may be the best example. The Polish economy seems to be in good shape. Moreover, there is now substantial foreign investment in Poland. This is both ownership investment in privatized companies and investment in new companies and trading partners. Polish firms are able to raise money on international capital markets as well. Thus the sort of stock watering and managerial shirking observed in Russia (discussed in the next chapter) is not occurring in Poland (Miller *et al.* 1995).

Poland has a sufficiently developed legal system such that franchising as a business method is thriving. Franchisors are both European and American firms (Simpson 1995). There is also foreign investment in the Czech Republic (for example, Toy and Miller 1995). Moreover, foreign companies are finding sufficient certainty in all three countries so that there are substantial business links between Eastern and Western Europe, in the form of acquisitions, partnerships and supplier networks (Miller *et al.* 1994). George Soros, a successful investor in Eastern Europe, is described as 'generally upbeat' about the progress of these countries (Gordon 1995).

Thus the evidence from at least three of the former communist countries indicates that if correct measures are taken, then it is possible to emerge successfully from the desolation created by communism. One part of the required efforts includes creation or re-creation of a rule of

law, and these three countries have undertaken the investments needed
to do this.

6. Russia

Russia seems to have a less well-adapted body of law than the Czech Republic, Hungary or Poland. This may be because Russia was communist for a longer time than the others, so that existing pre-communist law is older than in the other countries and there are additional generations of people who have had no actual exposure to markets. Moreover, at the time of the Revolution, Russia was less economically advanced than were the other countries when they became communist. Indeed it was not an economy in any real sense of the term.

THE FORMAL LEGAL SYSTEM

The major legal weaknesses do not seem to be only in the area of contract law itself. There is a large body of Russian contract law which was used under the Soviet system to govern transactions between enterprises. This law differs from contract law in market economies. However, it is not as different as we might expect: 'More surprising, perhaps, is the substantial convergence of contractual norms in Soviet and Anglo-American legal systems despite significant differences in the organization of capitalist and socialist economies' (Kroll 1987, 147). Attorneys and businessmen in Russia indicated in private conversations that difficulties in doing business are due more to uncertainty about government actions than contractual weaknesses.

One example of forces leading to legal uncertainty in Russia is what has been called the 'war of laws'. Various levels of government may pass conflicting laws, and there is no mechanism for resolving such conflicts. This makes business planning difficult.

At the time of this writing, the problem of lack of clarity and uniformity exists at all levels of government and involves uncertainty concerning the location of authority to legislate and implement the laws, the nature and extent of the legislative and executive powers, and the appropriate means and methods for enforcement (IMF 1991, 226).

While the splitting of the Soviet Union into independent countries may have reduced these problems, it has not solved them all, and local laws are continually changing. There are inconsistencies in rules and interpretations of various ministries and departments of Russia. The multiplicity of fora for resolution of commercial disputes is more severe in economies that lack a well-developed body of commercial law because different courts may use different and inconsistent rules and laws.

There are over 800 ministries in Russia, and many of these can stop any given deal (Kvint 1993, 26). Obtaining approval from all relevant parties to undertake a deal has been called 'death by committee' (Poe 1993, 54). Building one property development in Moscow required permits from 130 different committees (Rossant 1994). This leads to possibilities of substantial corruption. Shleifer and Vishny (1993) indicate that the most dangerous form of corruption is that in which several authorities have the power to stop an activity, so that bribes must be paid to many potential enforcers and an actor cannot be certain that he has bribed all the relevant officials; they indicate that this is the case in Russia. Poe (1993, 236–7) describes the same situation. Mauro (1995) provides evidence that societies with more corruption invest less and grow more slowly. Erlanger (1995) also indicates that official corruption is an ongoing problem in Russia, and may be more of a detriment to investment than organized crime. An important theme of Handelman (1995) is that there may be little difference, and that there are close links between criminals and government officials.

The law used in the formal legal system in Russia has been inadequate in many dimensions. The basic commercial law in use until recently was a 1964 law. This was modified by many subsequent decrees and laws, but was nonetheless seriously incomplete. Moreover, there are inconsistencies among the various laws passed or adopted since the fall of communism. Thus the body of law governing commercial relationships is weak and difficult to use.

To quote one example, debt collection has been difficult (Dubik 1994a). Until recently, courts charged 10 per cent of the disputed sum; in October 1994 a decree reduced this amount and applied a sliding scale. Nonetheless, use of the courts is difficult. A legal proceeding can only be filed after a debt is three months overdue, and courts take two months or more to rule on cases. With high inflation, debt collection is problematical with such delays. The inflation rate was over 2500 per cent in 1992, over 800 per cent in 1993 and 200 per cent in 1994. It appears to be lower so far in 1995, but it is still high enough so that delayed debt collection is quite costly. While newer laws sometimes allow inflation adjustments or indexing, this was not always true in the past, and does not seem to be true in all cases even now.

Another example is the difficulty banks have had in seizing certain collateral for loans in default. As a result, loans have tended to be for short time periods, such as 90 days (Filipov 1994). On the other hand, the 29 May 1992 Russian mortgage law does allow for the use of real property as collateral for bank loans. Moreover, this law is quite flexible in allowing parties to choose whatever terms are most congenial (Osakwe 1993, 354–5). However, although there are six private mortgage registers, there is no central register where a lender can establish the priority of his mortgage (Levy 1995). More recently it has been reported that banks' rights to foreclose are still not defined. As a result, mortgages tend to be for short terms (no more than ten years, and often six months to one year with an option to renew). Down payments are high, typically 30–40 per cent. As of September 1995, only about 1000 mortgages have been reported (Banerjee and Teodorescu 1995).

An additional difficulty is that there are three separate court systems (Vlasihin 1993). There is a system of business courts, the arbitration courts (which is not an arbitration court in the Western sense), that hears disputes between businesses. However, if one party to a dispute is a private citizen, another court system is involved. There is yet another system, the Constitutional Court. It is not always clear which court will hear a particular dispute. Moreover, since there are three systems that might hear similar disputes, the rate of development of precedents and predictability of the law will be retarded. While there are potential benefits from competing court systems, this does not seem to be the case in Russia because the parties do not seem able to choose *ex ante* which system will govern their dispute.

Aslund (1995) also discusses difficulties in passing relevant laws. He suggests that the conflicts between the government and the Supreme Soviet, between the government and ministries remaining from the communist era, and between the central government and regional governments created great difficulties.

Even when laws are passed, problems remain. This is because of delays in passing relevant laws and inefficiencies that exist between the passage of laws. Even today, insufficient laws have been passed to enable the economy to function at a high level. As mentioned earlier, this may be a pervasive feature of a legal system based on codes when legal change is difficult and there are lags. I will discuss three major laws.

The 1990 Law 'On Property in Russia'

This law was seriously incomplete. The required subordinate legislation was delayed because of political difficulties, and much is still lacking Moreover: 'There was no clear distribution of state property between the Federation and its member republics, districts, and regions' (Topornin 1993, 17). These problems in allocation of property rights and conflict between governmental units still plague the country today; examples are provided below. It also appears that in Russia, more than in the other countries, there remain people in authority with some hostility towards the adoption of markets, and the number of such people appears to be increasing.

The 1992 Arbitration Procedural Code (APC)[12]

This established a nation-wide system of arbitration courts and provided rules for binding arbitration and enforcement. This law was a major improvement over the previous situation because it did provide more authority for arbitration. However, the APC was a procedural code, and it still depended on the existing body of substantive law. Some of the difficulties addressed by Greif and Kandel (1995) have been remedied by subsequent legislation (the 10 per cent fee for arbitration has been reduced and the legislature has recently passed a new substantive commercial law, as discussed below), but other problems – problems of competence of judges and lack of enforcement – remain. Moreover, the new Commercial Code does not mention arbitration at all.

The official arbitration courts suffer additional problems. For domestic disputes, the major court is the Supreme Arbitration Court.[13] The Arbitration Court is the basic commercial court in Russia. Yakovlev (1994) indicates that his court has difficulty in obtaining enforcement of its orders. He also indicates that the long delays in hearing disputes create severe problems. He blames the 'bloody squabbles' among entrepreneurs on the delays in using the court. Nineteen courts, including the Moscow court, do not have independent physical facilities. The judges in this court are the same as in the Soviet era and, because of low pay, many of the best have left (Black *et al.* 1995). Middle level judges earn only $160 per month and are largely dependent on the goodwill of others in the system for other benefits, such as housing (*Economist* 1995a, at 48).

Pistor (1995) indicates that the enforcement of private arbitration decrees is sometimes possible, particularly if assets are available in banks. However, there are risks, and she indicates that on occasion assets will be 'siphoned off by enforcers'. While the number of cases handled by the Arbitration Court has fallen by almost 30 per cent from 1993 to 1994, the number of debt collection cases has fallen by only 8 per cent, suggesting that users of courts are less unhappy with the courts as debt collectors than with other functions of the courts. She also indicates that the Arbitration Court has in general been willing to enforce awards from private arbitrators, and treats these orders as final and binding. Nonetheless, Pistor indicates that private arbitration courts are used very little. However, more optimistically, Langer and Buyevitch (1995) indicate that the number of cases heard by the International Arbitration Court of the Russian Federation Chamber of Commerce and Industry tripled from 1993 to 1994.

The Russian Arbitration Court attached to the Russian Chamber of Commerce and Industry (discussed in Viechtbauer 1993) handles international disputes. This court is descended from a Soviet court, the Foreign Trade Arbitration Court. However, there are numerous difficulties with this court as well. There is, 'limited availability of persons with the expertise necessary to qualify for the list of arbitrators' (p. 371). The court will not allow the parties to specify the law to govern a dispute; only court rules will be followed (p. 401). Enforcement of awards is difficult and not automatic (p. 420). As a result, relatively few disputes are brought to this court; Western businesses are more likely to name third country (often Swedish) arbitrators. Nonetheless, this court has the most experience in Russia of capitalist economic dealings. It is also beginning to publish its most important decisions, so that disputants may be able to determine in advance the likely outcome of an arbitration. This may also be a step towards a more common law-like process in Russia, as advocated earlier.

The 1995 Commercial Code

A newly adopted Commercial Code came into effect on 1 January 1995 (Russian Federation 1994). This consolidated and updated many laws, so that the law actually in use will be greatly improved. The new code is a definite advance over previous law. One severe problem has been inflation. In the past, with very high inflation rates, the value of settlements decreased substantially as there were delays in collection. Parts of the new code may address this issue. Article 337 says that, 'a pledge shall secure a demand in that amount which it has at the moment of satisfaction, in particular, interest, compensation of losses caused by delay of performance', and this may be interpreted as allowing some inflation adjustment. Payments for 'Maintenance of Citizen' (apparently compensation for lost wages and earnings) will be indexed with the minimum wage ('amount of payment for labour established by law': Article 319). On the other hand, the section on Bankruptcy of an Entrepreneur (Article 25) makes no similar provisions. Since bankruptcy is often used as a method of debt collection, this lack may be costly.[14]

However, the new code is by no means a panacea. Many difficulties remain. First, the judges are the same, and one serious problem with the legal system is the competence and ability of judges. Second, many problems stem from difficulties in enforcing decrees and rulings of the courts, and enforcement problems also remain. Third, while Article 11 indicates that there are three types of court, it does nothing to clarify their relationship. Fourth, there is an insufficient number of lawyers in Russia. Most Soviet era lawyers were criminal lawyers, and there were relatively few of them. Now there are too few lawyers for a large market economy and relatively few of these lawyers are skilled in commercial matters (Siltchenkov 1993). There are only 20,000 independent lawyers in Russia, and 28,000 public prosecutors. Although the USA has too many lawyers, Russia has only one-eighth as many (*Economist* 1995a, at 43).

Finally, the entire code is only 127 pages long and deals with several areas of law, including all of contract law, property law and the law of business associations. This means that there are of necessity large ambiguities in the law, and thus parties will remain uncertain about outcomes of litigation. It is planned that future parts of the code will correct some of these ambiguities, but they have yet to be written or adopted. Unless Russian courts are willing to adopt some sort of common law-type system to codify interpretations of the law, it will be difficult for litigants to predict the outcome of cases. To its credit, the law does indicate that in the event of interpretive uncertainty, the outcome of a dispute, 'shall be determined by the customs of business turnover applicable to the relations of the parties' (Article 419).

Thus while the revision in the Commercial Code is useful and needed, nonetheless, even after this revision, difficulties will remain.[15]

LEGAL FAILURES: EXAMPLES

Even if the law were well developed, the state would be required for enforcement. As indicated above, there is little evidence that the state is providing sufficient enforcement of contracts, even in those cases where there are court rulings. In addition, to establish credibility as an enforcer, it would be necessary for the state to hold itself to its own agreements. There is evidence that willingness to do so is lacking. Part of the problem is that there are several levels of government, and the central government may be lacking sufficient power to compel lower level governments to honour their agreements. A common pattern is for the government to offer terms to a foreign investor to induce specific investments in Russia and then opportunistically to change the terms so as to appropriate some or all of the quasi-rents associated with the investment.

Attorneys and others complain that new laws are passed with no thought to their consistency with existing law. This problem seems to be continuing. However, although numerous inconsistent and inefficient laws are passed, the lack of enforcement and implementation may serve to mitigate some of the problems created (Fogel 1995a). There are no legal provisions for ending joint ventures and allocating their property, so some potential transactors are reluctant to form such ventures. One strategy for dealing with such legal inconsistency is to enter the market on a small scale and observe what happens. Many foreign firms, for example, have small investments in Russia, often involving only the retailing of products. Poe (1993) recommends a similar strategy in determining the reliability of a potential Russian partner. To the extent that quicker or larger investments would occur if there were increased certainty, then the uncertainty is imposing real costs on the Russian economy.

Only 8 per cent of potential joint ventures begin operating (Kvint 1993, 181). Kvint estimates that 10 per cent of the failures of joint ventures are due to legal problems, 28 per cent to an inability to find an appropriate partner and 20 per cent to 'financing'. These difficulties may be exacerbated by legal problems. For example, difficulty in finding financing may be caused by poor property rights definitions or difficulty in foreclosing, making it difficult to use property as collateral. Finding a partner may be made more difficult because of contractual uncertainty. Thus the legal system may be responsible for a greater percentage of failures than is immediately apparent. Sixteen per cent of the failures are due to 'bureaucratic problems' that may also relate to legal uncertainty.

In one (randomly selected) week in May, 1993, the *Moscow Times*, a daily English language newspaper, reported the following examples of market interference and contractual uncertainty:[16]

From 9 April to 25 May, oil prices were controlled at levels well below market prices as a result of a politically motivated decree imposed before the election. As a result, Moscow suffered severe gasoline shortages. Some refineries had refused to sell in Moscow; two refineries had closed down. Even though the price was to rise, the new controlled price was 75 rubles per litre, while mobile tanks were already selling gasoline for 120 to 150 rubles per litre.

A Korean–Russian joint venture had invested $70 million in a timber project in eastern Russia since 1990. An environmental dispute went to the Russian Supreme Court which, 'failed to come to any concrete conclusion, sending the case back to the regional court'. There has also been a 'worsening tax situation'. While it was originally estimated that the venture would earn a profit by the fourth year, 'under current conditions it could take seven to 10 years'. Other potential investors are monitoring this situation closely.

De Beers had signed a five year contract with the Russian diamond marketing agency; now the 'Precious Metals and Stones Committee' is attempting to renegotiate this contract.

The Moscow city government changed the method of taxing land owned by joint ventures. Previously tax was paid at the same rate as that paid by Russians (about $3500 per hectare). Now the rate will range up to $465,000 per hectare, the rate paid by foreigners:

> The new decree is the latest in a series of changes in tax and landownership laws that have made it difficult for foreign and Russian firms to lease property for office space and development in the capital. In recent months, for example, the City Council has annulled leases signed by the mayor's office and passed legislation calling for lease agreements to be renegotiated.

These new tax rates mean that some past investments may not be profitable, and many would not have been undertaken.

Other examples can be cited from Tourevski and Morgan (1993): The Ministry of Foreign Economic Relations is creating an auditing board that will have the right to control or even shut down any independent entity engaged in foreign economic relations, and will be able to question the business decisions of entities subject to its control. Russian customs officials and later the KGB seized automobile batteries produced by an American–Russian joint venture because of a technicality in the joint venture charter. Customs officials refused permission for a Leningrad company to export scrap metal, even though the company had permission from the Russian Federation. A cooperative began to recover and process timber that had sunk during the process of floating it downstream and that otherwise was wasted. Within six months, the government shut down the operation, so that the timber continues to be wasted. A Russian magazine publisher contracted to trade waste paper for computers. However, it was denied a licence to export waste. Galuszka and Chandler (1995) indicate that there are additional problems with joint ventures. However, they also suggest that because of legal changes, joint ventures are no longer being formed as commonly as before, and that foreign companies investing directly in Russia have fewer difficulties.

Western oil companies might spend up to $70 billion annually to develop Russian oil fields were it not for fears of opportunism (Imse 1993). Much of this opportunism is by the government, which seems often to change rules or to increase export taxes in a way designed opportunistically to appropriate past investments. There is private opportunism as well. After one company had invested in machinery for drilling for Russian oil, the firm controlling the pipeline that provided the only route to the sea doubled its rates.

The Raddison Corporation negotiated an agreement with the Kremlin to build a hotel in Moscow. However, once the property was completed, Moscow city council demanded a partnership before allowing the hotel to open. Negotiations delayed the opening for about one year, and the city did get a partnership (Thomas and Sutherland 1992, 147).

Even where investment does occur, investors are aware that contracts are subject to great political uncertainty. Elf Aquitane, the French company, has signed a contract to explore for oil in Russia and Kazakhstan (Salpukas 1993). Other American oil companies have also signed contracts, but Elf's endeavour is the only one that is not part of a joint venture:

> Elf has the first of what is called a production agreement with Russia...but whether the contract will remain in effect as written remains uncertain...It took Elf about a year to get the deal approved by the Russian Parliament, but whether this gives the contract any legal force is still murky, given the struggle between President Boris Yeltsin and some leaders of the Parlia-

ment...A high official in the Tyumen Region, Russia's largest oil area, said there was a continuing tug of war between local officials and the ministers in Moscow over control of new ventures...In such an atmosphere, Elf's straightforward contract could be bent out of shape.[17]

Ikea, the Swedish furniture company, did plan to invest in producing goods as well as selling in Russia. In 1988, Ikea agreed to renovate a dozen Russian furniture factories to produce furniture that it planned to sell in stores it planned to open by 1991. However, the plan failed when the USSR collapsed. Ikea is involved in litigation and in arbitration in Stockholm. Ikea's Chief Executive, Anders Moberg, has been quoted as saying: 'Terrible problems untangling various obligations between the old USSR and the new republics have us much more cautious'. Ikea now plans to invest in Poland, Hungary and the Czech and Slovak Republics, but not in Russia (Moore 1993).

Komineft, a major Russian oil company, diluted its stock by about one-third without telling many stockholders, including foreign investors. However, the secret issue was ultimately reversed and the company agreed to move its shareholder register to Moscow (Banerjee (1995a), *Moscow Times* (1995)). Primorsky Sea Shipping recently doubled its number of shares and sold them to a subsidiary for $90,000, although the value of the firm was $36 million. Two other Russian shipping companies have undertaken similar transactions. So far, such transactions have been held to be legal (Liesman 1995a,b). Lebedinsky Mining Company diluted Rossisky Credit Bank's shares (Galuszka and Kranz 1995). However, one Russian investment fund was successful in replacing the management of Yaroslav Rubber Company (Galuszka and Kranz 1995).

White Nights is a joint venture formed to increase production from existing Russian oil fields (Goldman 1994). After the venture was formed, the Russians increased taxes several times and also required additional investments from the American partners. Goldman (p. 248) indicates that: 'Had they known there would have been such a confiscatory tax, the American partners would probably have negotiated different terms or not signed the contract at all'. Thus this is a classic example of *ex-post* opportunism, as quasi-rent extraction (Rubin 1990).

This seems to be continuing. Chevron is reducing its investment in Kazakhstan and Pennzoil and Gulf Canada resources, Inc. are trying to sell their investments, in part because of 'political chaos and onerous taxes'. One company that set up a joint venture has 'been hit by no fewer than 40 new regulations and taxes' and is almost bankrupt

(Liesman and du Bois 1995). Western investors in oil were originally told they could export the oil, but later were subject to export taxes, quotas and regulations. Export quotas change from month to month. One Western investor says that, 'Russian export and tax laws change with the wind' (Fogel and Reifenberg 1995). Lobbying, however, seems to be effective in muting the costs of some regulations: the oil quotas have been relaxed as a result of lobbying by oil producers (Fogel 1995a). On the other hand, Conoco has successfully developed an oil processing facility and pipeline, and is shipping oil. The return on investment so far is small, but the company views it as a learning mechanism. However, the venture will remain profitable only so long as a tax exemption on the oil export tax remains in effect (Galuszka 1994).

Prime Minister Chernomyrdin promised in the summer of 1994 that laws were in process to exempt foreign business from certain changes in law, but these had not been introduced by April 1995 (Craik 1995). Indeed a law that went into effect on 15 March 1995 removed several tax breaks that foreign investors had previously been promised (Mileusnic 1995a). Many firms planned investment strategies based on a December 1993 presidential decree exempting certain in-kind capital imports from a VAT; the new law may remove that exemption.

On 29 March 1995 the government announced that certain Western offices ('representative' offices, often used as an unprofitable first step to entering the Russian market) would be subject to a 35 per cent additional payroll tax on monthly wages above $25, and that this tax would be retroactive to 1 January 1994. Previously these offices had been exempt from this tax (Fogel 1995b; Galuszka and Dallas 1995). Officials removed a tax exemption on imported construction materials, leading to another large retroactive tax increase. Moreover, taxes often carry retroactive penalties of up to three times the tax itself (Galuszka and Dallas 1995). The capriciousness of the tax system discourages investment and makes planning difficult.

One effect of legal uncertainty is a high cost of doing business. Liesman (1995c) indicates that the rental for office space in Moscow is among the highest in the world, equivalent to rentals in Tokyo or New York. The explanation for such high rates seems to be risk. Much construction seems to be begun and then stopped because of, 'financing questions or problems with the bureaucratic city approval process'. Thus given these risks, rents must be high to compensate builders. These high rents then increase the cost of doing business in Moscow.

Widespread smuggling also creates difficulties (Winestock 1995). Firms that have paid import duties find themselves underpriced by smugglers. Moreover, high officials sometimes grant exemptions to favoured firms, allowing them legally to import with reduced taxes. Yeltsin has granted exemptions from import duties to the National Sports Fund, which now imports 60–80 per cent of all tobacco and alcohol. As a result, firms with no exemptions are less likely to import into the Russian market.

Tourevski and Morgan (1993, 166–7) indicate several areas in which respondents to interviews (Russian and foreign businessmen) have indicated weakness in the law. Indeed this weakness is a major theme of the book. Some problems with law are: vague, contradictory, inconsistent formulations; isolated law-making, divorced from international legislation; conflict between laws which had been centralized and the republics, between the republics themselves, or between the republics and their autonomous territories; and the instability of laws which are unclear and change from day to day.

A formal recent survey of investors has indicated the extent of the problems associated with an ineffective legal system (Craik 1995; Halligan and Teplukin 1995). According to the survey, the 'most important restraints to investment' are, 'fear for shareholder rights and weak contract law'. The story reporting the results of the survey begins: 'Russia's ever-shifting and poorly enforced legal system is by far the biggest single impediment to a much-needed investment boom that could provide the impetus for reform, a survey of domestic and international businesses operating here shows'.

Taxation, which reflects the fear of opportunism, is the second major reason for not investing in Russia. There is also an inability to find suitable business partners, reflecting the amount of uncertainty in the Russian economy and the unwillingness of firms to create valuable reputations. The survey is particularly significant since it indicates that even those businesses that have invested in Russia find the legal system an impediment. Presumably it has been even more of an impediment to those businesses that have considered such investment but decided against it. Indeed the level of investment in Russia is falling.

The survey indicates that the main legal problem is the difficulty of enforcing stock market investments, because of problems with share registers, such as those discussed above with respect to Komineft and Primorsky. The second major concern was contract law, 'which was seen as complex and difficult to implement'. Respondents indicate that the Civil Code has made an improvement but, 'businesses say that in practice, many courts lack the expertise to implement the system'. Apparently, broken promises by the government itself (as discussed in more detail below) are counted as part of the difficulty with contract law.

'Political instability' rated as only the third most serious concern. However, viewed in the framework adopted here, it may be that political instability, by reducing time horizons, has itself created some of the difficulties in establishing the needed certainty for contract law to function well. Fear of a lack of commitment to capitalism on the part of the government is the greatest political fear identified in the survey, and fear of renationalization is second. These fears are a major factor in creating the high discount rates that lead to the other identified problems.

Recently, the Executive Director of the Russian Securities Commission has defended the investment climate in Russia (Vasiliev 1995). However, as of July 1995, the strongest arguments made are that, 'regulations *now being written* will govern all aspects of market activity' and, '*soon*, the Securities Commission will also have formal enforcement mechanisms at its disposal' (emphasis added). Vasiliev does claim that some companies have adequately protected shareholder rights, but the example given (the Red October chocolate factory) is a company needing additional capital. However, the *Economist* (1995a) does indicate that several reforms are being planned or implemented to make the Russian stock market more reliable. Kranz (1995b) indicates that there are institutions that register shares, such as the Moscow Central Depository, and that Chase Manhattan Bank has a cooperative arrangement with this organization. She indicates that certainty and stability in the stock market are increasing (1995a,b). Liesman (1995d) indicates that, as of October 1995, American investors were reluctant to invest in Russia, in part because new securities, tax reform and corporate laws promised by the government had not yet been passed. Articles in the US business press sometimes advise against investing in Russia (for example, Dunkin 1995).

POLITICAL BASES FOR LEGAL UNCERTAINTY

These examples indicate difficulties with the political system of Russia, rather than with the legal system itself. In order for such problems to be corrected, political reform is needed. The sort of remedies proposed in this work are only available in economies where those with political power have the will to impose reforms; they cannot be used where such will is lacking.

Political stability will support legal reform in another way. Part of the difficulty with contract enforcement is caused by uncertainty. Many of the mechanisms discussed here depend on reputations and on other long-term investments (for example, in self-enforcing agreements). If parties believe that legal or property institutions are likely to change in the near future, they will be willing to invest less in such agreements. This may explain the widely noted tendency of Russian negotiators to drive excessively difficult bargains, discussed above. Such bargaining may mean that the Russian participants receive lower long-term returns from the agreement, but if parties have short time horizons this will be less significant.

Short time horizons may also explain some otherwise puzzling behaviour of political authorities. If a political authority radically changes the tax rate faced by businesses, then this can be profitable in the short run because the jurisdiction can appropriate the quasi-rents from the completed investment. However, this policy has long-term costs because other businesses will be less willing to invest in this jurisdiction. But a short time horizon means that the present value of the appropriated investments can outweigh the long-term losses from lost future investments.

Again the problem is uncertainty. If governments breach agreements, they can expect greatly reduced future investment as other potential investors refrain from investing. However, if the relevant officials do not expect the government to last, there is less cost from opportunism and such appropriation becomes more likely. Other potential transactors, observing that the state does not even honour its own agreements, would understandably place relatively little weight on the state as a neutral enforcer of other contracts.[18] Cowley (1995) indicates that this uncertainty has caused the market to place low values on Russian assets. For example, a barrel of oil owned by a Western company is valued at $5.50; by a Russian company, at $0.10. Boettke (1995) indicates that this uncertainty about the stability of government policies and commitment of the government to particular reforms is a continuation of similar uncertainty from the Soviet era. Since such uncertainty and unpredictability have a long history in Russia, it may be difficult to convince the people that any given policy or reform will be stable.

The Coase theorem (Coase 1960) shows that with well-defined property rights and sufficiently low transaction costs, the final use of resources is efficient and invariant with respect to initial rights assignments. Most criticisms of the theorem have focused on the second condition – the magnitude of transaction costs. However, the situation in Russia today is one in which the theorem may not hold because the first condition, the existence of well-defined property rights, is not satisfied. The problem is not anarchy; the situation may be worse than in anarchy. Rather it is the existence of too many governments, with lines of power insufficiently well defined between them. Property rights are not well defined because it is not clear who has the power to define them. The result is that resources will not be used efficiently. It is essential that this problem is solved for any degree of economic progress to be feasible.

For private enforcement mechanisms to function requires investments of exactly the sort that may not be worthwhile given the levels of uncertainty in Russia today. Required investments are of several sorts. The simplest is investment in reputation for honesty. By demonstrating a willingness to refrain from exploiting a situation to its fullest (as, for example, by not offering high quality and supplying low quality goods when detection of quality is impossible before purchase), a firm can establish a reputation for honesty. However, this investment will pay only with sufficiently low discount rates. Otherwise the gains from exploiting the immediate situation will outweigh the gains from greater future profits.

Similarly, self-enforcing agreements work only because the present value of future profits from the expected sequence of exchanges between two parties is greater than the immediate gains from cheating. This again is a form of investment and requires sufficiently low discount rates to make the agreement actually self-enforcing.

It is important to separate multilateral mechanisms that are open to any member from those based on religious or ethnic solidarity (Landa 1981). The traditional pattern of trade in Russia has been based on such ethnic or cultural groups. Greif (1994) indicates that this pattern of trade is associated with 'collectivist' as opposed to 'individualist' culture, and that the latter is more common in developed economies. Here I am concerned with individualist associations, that is, those not based on personal relationships. While groups based on ethnic solidarity are useful for some purposes, such groups enable trade to occur only between members. Valuable transactions with non-members become impossible, and therefore resources are unable to flow to their highest valued use. (Such ethnic solidarity is also often the basis for criminal gangs, in Russia and elsewhere, for the same reason: contract enforcement by courts is unavailable to criminals.)

The argument advanced here has both normative and positive implications for Russia. The normative implication is that agents should form groups based on characteristics other than ethnic solidarity. Businesses should actively seek to generate such organizations, and advisers to businesses should suggest the formation of such associations. Governments should facilitate the formation of groups engaging in multilateral enforcement. Such facilitation should be active, as by passing laws encouraging the formation of multilateral enforcement mechanisms. The most important such law would be to agree to enforce private arbitration decisions where the parties have agreed to voluntary arbitration. Government should provide passive support, as by not over-zealously applying antitrust laws to such groups. The new Russian Commercial Code does indicate that: 'The creation of associations of commercial and/or non-commercial organizations in the form of associations (or unions) shall be permitted' (Article 50). This means that there is a possibility for such multilateral enforcement organizations to form.

The positive implication is that we should expect to observe spontaneous formation of associations applying the sort of enforcement mechanisms discussed above. That is, we would expect to observe voluntary formation of trade associations and other groups whose purpose is enforcement of agreements in exactly the ways discussed above. We would expect two types of such organization. First, groups analogous to trade associations would be expected to govern relations between firms in an industry. Members of such groups should be firms in the industry. Second, there should be groups of firms in different industries within a geographic region. These organizations should govern relations between member firms and consumers or suppliers who are not in the same industry. These would be analogous to US Better Business Bureaus, but with more enforcement power with respect to members. I have information on several groups of the second sort – those dealing with several businesses in a given geographic area.

PRIVATE MECHANISMS: EXAMPLES

Self-Regulatory Broker Associations

Regional trading associations of brokers have been established with the encouragement of the recently empowered Russian Federation Commission on Securities and Exchanges and with the assistance of US government-financed resident advisers. These associations will be self-regulating, with a director of enforcement and compliance rules based on US and international standards. So far, four have been established.

These groups have compliance rules and a director of enforcement. It is intended that complaints will be heard by a panel that has the power to issue various sanctions, including publicity, warnings, fines, restitution and suspension or expulsion of the violating member. There is also a possibility of arbitration (called 'the committee to settle disputes' since 'arbitration' has a different meaning in Russian law). However, there appears to be some reluctance to apply the expected sanctions for breach of agreement with respect to the first complaints in the Moscow association. Thus a group exists, as predicted, but so far has been unwilling to apply the expected sanctions for breach of agreements. Mileusnic (1995b) indicates that the Duma has removed the provision allowing self-enforcement from the current draft securities law, perhaps to facilitate bribes to government enforcers. Rulings such as these can do nothing but harm.

Shareholder Rights

Seven large industrial firms and investment funds have recently signed an agreement with respect to shareholder rights (Dubik 1994b). These firms have agreed to provide detailed audited financial information to shareholders and to have independent managers maintain possession and control of shareholder registers so that shareholders can be guaranteed that their holdings will indeed be registered. The agreement bans insider trading and regulates voting by shareholders. The method of enforcement is unclear, but presumably, since the promises of the firms relate to public activities, expulsion from the association would be simple.

Such self-regulatory organizations seem to be having some positive effects. At least three associations (the Association of Broker-Dealers, the League of Investment Funds and the Russian Association of Investment Funds) have been established and undertake some self-policing. For example, when one fund went bankrupt as a result of fraud by management, the League of Investment Funds took it over and has generated some returns for investors. The Association of Broker-Dealers is arbitrating a dispute between two large firms, Troika Dialog and First Voucher Investment Fund (Banerjee 1995b). This is particularly important because the court system has apparently failed to resolve this dispute (Tolkacheva 1995).

On the other hand, significant problems with shareholder rights still exist and investors view these as being highly troublesome, as discussed above. Some firms have refused to list new investors as stockholders, or to allow them to attend meetings. More recently, some firms have unilaterally diluted investments. Managers as lobbyists and members of parliament have succeeded in blocking much legislation that would address this problem (Liesman 1995b). In a survey of 27 Russian privatized firms, Gurkov and Asselbergs (1995, 209) find that managers in all cases have, 'developed several effective mechanisms to ensure their total control over company assets'. The appearance is that determinedly opportunistic firms will be able to devise mechanisms to expropriate investments. This will deter investment. Firms needing capital have refrained from such behaviour, but other firms have not (Liesman 1995b; see also Black *et al.* 1995).

Commodities Exchanges

One class agency that does perform exactly the functions identified above is the 'commodities exchange'. These are trading centres, with many firms as members. Zhurek (1993, 42) indicates that the International Food Exchange offers a variety of services, including, 'arbitration for the rapid settlement of trade disputes'. Volume on this exchange is low, but the Moscow Commodities Exchange did over $500 million in business in May 1991 (Thomas and Sutherland 1992, 136).

There are at least 165 commodities exchanges in Russia and 20 in Moscow (Wegren 1994). Participants understand that methods of dispute resolution between participants are necessary. Moreover, most exchanges require a recommendation from two members and an examination of financial and reputational capital before admitting a new member. However, there does not seem to be a strong system of enforcement of promises. Contracts are often not honoured and payments are often not made. In 1992, approximately 30 per cent of contracts were not fulfilled.

Brokers will sometimes offer their wares on several exchanges and choose the best deal, paying a small fine to the exchanges where promises have been broken. This appears to be because of weaknesses in the exchanges themselves. Buyers and sellers often use the exchange to establish contacts, but conclude deals 'on the side' in order to avoid paying the commission to the exchange and to avoid taxes. Thus while these exchanges would be in a position to enforce agreements if they could govern trade, they seem to be too weak to do so under current conditions. Frye (1995) indicates that members are unwilling to use arbitration courts associated with the exchanges because this would require providing public information about trades that would make taxation of the trades easy.

Additional Mechanisms

Greif and Kandel (1995) report on several related mechanisms. There are several private arbitration courts, including courts set up by commodities exchanges, banking associations and the Bar Association. In 1993 over 100 companies (Russian and foreign) each paid a fee to establish the Moscow Commercial Court, a permanent arbitration committee. The Moscow Arbitration Court will enforce its decisions. Additionally, 'business groups' are associations of businessmen that join together for one-time deals. However, members will engage in several such deals over time. If anyone reneges, they will be prohibited from participating in future deals. These voluntary groups based on multiple interlocking transactions are not cultural or ethnic groups, but they do have common interests and a common code of behaviour.

Cooperatives in Russia have formed two types of association for lobbying purposes (Jones and Moskoff 1991). Some are geographically organized, and include businesses in a particular area. Others are essentially trade associations and include cooperatives in the same business sector. Associations of cooperatives provide services to members, including legal assistance, and pursue a political programme. Two major organizations are the USSR Union of Amalgamated Cooperatives (founded in 1989) and the Union of Leaseholders and Entrepreneurs (1990) (Jones 1992). Representatives of the cooperative movement were involved in decision-making regarding legislation. Again, these structures correspond to the types of potential multilateral organization discussed above, but there is no evidence that these organizations presently perform such functions.

Tourevski and Morgan (1993) indicate that the Soviet Chamber of Commerce has begun performing an information function. This organization publishes a directory regarding foreign trade participants, including information about financial positions and business reputations. Other organizations perform similar functions. Some private organizations also provide such business information. The accounting firm of Ernst & Young has established a joint venture that provides information about various aspects of doing business, including information about 'reliability of the partners' and several other private ventures are providing such information. However, Tourevski and Morgan believe that there is a dearth of useful business information. This has been exacerbated because for a time Soviet private firms were prohibited from performing 'middleman' functions.

Moreover, a fear of organized crime may contribute to the unwillingness of firms to provide public information. The head of one association, the Russian Business Round Table, has recently been poisoned. His associates indicate that the motive may have been the unwillingness of the Association to allow criminal firms to join (Stanley 1995). More generally, any public information useful for establishing a reputation can be used by criminals to target profitable or successful firms for purposes of extortion. This is only one aspect of the danger to the Russian economy from criminal enterprises.

CRIMINALS AS ENFORCERS?

It may be that criminals will act as enforcers for contracts. Leitzel *et al.* (1995) claim that the 'main benefit' of the Mafia is contract enforcement. Similarly, Erlanger (1994) says that, 'the inability to get redress through the courts leads to more crime, as businesses hire muscle to enforce deals otherwise unenforceable'. Black *et al.* (1995, 21–2) indicate that violence is a real option in enforcement of corporate law. Aslund (1995, 169) also suggests that, 'banks take recourse to using gangsters, who force people to pay under threat of physical harm'. Kranz (1995a) indicates that, 'with the judicial system in shambles...Guns, bombs and grenades take the place of arbitration courts'.

On the other hand, Greif and Kandel (1995, 308) indicate that: 'There is no evidence that gangs actively enforced contracts except in those cases that directly concerned their interests'. (Leitzel *et al.* provide no evidence for their claim and neither do Black *et al*.) Greif and Kandel do indicate (p. 316) that with respect to security firms, 'contract enforcement on their part would be natural'. Handelman (1995) discusses the role of criminals as debt collectors at various places in his study of organized crime in Russia (for example, pp. 69, 168). However, whenever he mentions the debt collection function of thugs, he also indicates that they 'stave off unfriendly creditors' and 'intimidate creditors' so that there may be no net effect. Handelman indicates that gangsters have become associated with many firms, and that such associations are a normal and necessary part of doing business in Russia.[19] Such associations would be consistent with the claim of Greif and Kandel, that criminals collect only their own debts. Kranz (1995a) indicates that 40,000 enterprises in Russia may have Mafia connections, and that the Mafia sometimes infiltrates big business by first extending loans and then demanding management control.

Aslund (1995, 169–70) indicates that one-third of bank employees are security guards, indicating that banks either use these guards to fight the Mafia or that banks are 'infested with the Mafia'. Kranz (1995a) indicates that criminals sometimes try to take over companies by taking control of the company's bank, and that, 'as many as 10 of Russia's big banks may also have Mafia connections'.

However, while data are obviously lacking, there are reasons to doubt that the Mafia will actually provide an efficient level of contract enforcement. In particular, the discount rate is again relevant. A criminal gang hired to collect a debt has two options: keep the entire debt or turn over the contractual share to the original creditor. Which strategy is optimal depends on the discount rate. If this is high enough, then the gang may forgo the future gains from additional enforcement contracts and simply keep the money (or even extort additional money). If discount rates are sufficiently high, then creditors, expecting criminals to keep the debt, will not hire them and there will not be contractual enforcement by criminals.

Intriligator (1994) argues that the Mafias have very short time horizons. (He also claims that criminalization is destroying the Russian economy.) Even Leitzel *et al*. (1995), who are more optimistic regarding the role of the Mafia than Intriligator, believe that the mafiosi have short time horizons because of uncertainty. Handelman's suggestion that criminals are equity owners in many firms and Kranz's (1995a) discussion of this issue are consistent with this argument. Aslund (1995) is overall optimistic about the future of Russia, but even he admits

(p. 171) that, 'if no serious action is taken [with respect to crime], the legitimacy of democratic rule will be undermined'.

RUSSIA: SUMMARY

The evidence cited here is largely anecdotal. Data are lacking for a more systematic examination of the issues. However, potential investors in Russia are confronted with the same problem, and the data used here may be similar to the data used by such investors. As indicated above, the problems identified are the same as the problems that investors consider in making decisions about future commitments (Craik 1995; Halligan and Teplukin 1995).

There is insufficient ability to enforce contracts in Russia today. The law is weak, and even when decisions are obtained from courts, enforcement of decisions is often difficult. As a result, parties use private mechanisms for such enforcement. However, the power of such mechanisms is also weak. Firms have not yet established valuable reputations, so that they do not have valuable reputation capital to use to guarantee agreements. There are barriers to creation of such reputations, in the form of fear of expropriation by criminals or by tax collectors, or by corrupt officials. Some multilateral enforcement organizations have been formed, and these are aware of the problems associated with contract enforcement. However, many of them do not seem willing or able actually to take the steps needed to enforce agreements.

What does this mean? Things are bad, but perhaps improving. The question is, will they improve fast enough to enable Russia to become a fully developed economy, or will the economy remain trapped in a low level institutional equilibrium? We know from the examples of the Czech Republic, Hungary and Poland that it is possible for an economy to emerge successfully from the wasteland created by communism. However, since the situation is unique in human history, I cannot at this time predict if Russia will succeed or not. Greif's (1994) argument that collectivist cultures are less likely to be economically developed is one piece of evidence that would lead to pessimism, but it is by no means definitive. The December 1995 elections do not suggest optimism.

The true danger may be that if the legal system cannot function, then the criminal underground may become more and more powerful in both market and non-market activities (Erlanger 1994; Intriligator 1994; Handelman 1995; Kranz 1995a). Jeffrey Sachs (1995), a former adviser to the Russian government, indicates that 'Russia's corruption is singularly deep' and appears pessimistic about the future. George Soros, a well-known successful investor in Eastern Europe, indicates that, although he is investing in Russia because of the potential return, he is 'cautiously pessimistic' about the country. He believes the country is dominated by 'robber capitalism', defined as a 'breakdown of legal and financial controls', and that the economy is characterized as a struggle between rival gangs, including the communists as one such gang (Gordon 1995).[20]

On the other hand, Aslund (1994, 1995) believes that Russia is on the road to a successful transition. Galuszka *et al.* (1994), in a special *Business Week* report, indicate optimism and suggest that Russia has begun to develop and is no longer in danger of collapse. Poe (1993) believes that Russia will prosper, and his book (aimed at potential American investors in Russia) refers in its title to the 'Coming Russian Boom'. But Tourevski and Morgan (1993) and Kvint (1993) in books aimed at the same audience are less optimistic.

As I have stressed throughout, the issue is predictability. If the system becomes sufficiently stable and predictable to make investment in the creation of a rule of law and a set of contract-enforcing institutions worthwhile, then the problems I have discussed will be solved. If this happens, then I believe that the other problems facing the Russian economy will also become manageable. If the system continues to be unpredictable and if agents continue to lack faith in the future, then the problems will persist. At this time I cannot determine which will happen. Agnosticism is appropriate.

The situation in Russia is perhaps typical of what Tainter (1988, 19–20) indicates commonly occurs after the collapse of a complex society:

> With disintegration, central direction is no longer possible. The former political center undergoes a significant loss of prominence and power. It is often ransacked and may ultimately be abandoned. Small, petty states emerge in the formerly unified territory, of which the former capital may be one. Quite often these contend for domination, so that a period of perpetual conflict ensues. The umbrella of law and protection erected over the populace is eliminated. Lawlessness may prevail for a time...but order will ultimately be restored.[21]

Although the collapse of the Soviet Union fulfils many of the conditions discussed by Tainter, one may hope that Russia can avoid the most grim of these ramifications.

7. Government Policy

So far I have discussed private actions to create mechanisms for private enforcement. However, government can facilitate these mechanisms in various ways. Such facilitation can have two beneficial effects. First, by increasing the ability of agents to enter into agreements, the amount of beneficial transactions can increase. Second, by choice of proper policies, government can facilitate the creation of a body of precedent that can ultimately be used to create the beginnings of an efficient body of law.

I have in mind the following rough institutional structure. There is a court system in existence. This system has some rough notion of contract law. It may, for example, believe in 'freedom of contract' and in allowing voluntary private exchanges. However, there is not a complete body of contract law in place, so that decisions of the court system in resolving actual disputes will be somewhat uncertain.

In addition, it is likely that there are delays in reaching the court system. In a world of high inflation, these delays may be particularly costly if court awards are made in nominal currency units, which may be happening in Russia (private comment of Harold Berman). Unindexed contracts and court unwillingness to alter contractual terms were responsible for an epidemic of non-payment in inter-war Germany (Wolf 1993). Thus other mechanisms may be chosen where feasible.

In this section, I deal with two types of policy. Some policies will facilitate the formation of private agreements. However, it is also possible for incorrect government policies to penalize efficient conduct. Judging from past experience in the USA, misuse of antitrust policies is particularly likely to be costly. Even in the USA antitrust has often erred and punished pro-competitive conduct. In post-communist economies, where there may be an excessive fear of 'monopoly capitalism', such misuse may be particularly likely. All relevant antitrust statutes contain provisions that could lead to inefficient rulings (Pittman 1992; Gray and Associates 1993).

Of course, in analysing efficient government policy there is the issue of whether the government actually wants to adopt such policies. Efficient private law policies such as those discussed in this work may be easier to adopt than public law policies, because the role of interest groups is reduced in private law policies. This issue is discussed in more detail in the final chapter. Here I assume that the government wants efficient policies, and discuss their nature.

I analyse policy in the same tripartite framework used for analysing private enforcement mechanisms.

UNILATERAL MECHANISMS

The most important assistance governments can give to private firms for the creation of reputation capital is a willingness to enforce property rights in trademarks. Trademarks allow buyers to determine the quality of purchased goods and therefore enable sellers to invest in provision of high quality. All countries studied seem to have more or less appropriate trademark law on the books, but enforcement is uncertain and penalties may be inadequate.

If counterfeiting and trademark infringement are not sufficiently penalized, then there will be reduced incentives for firms to invest in brand name capital. Given that law enforcement authorities apparently lack adequate resources optimally to enforce laws against counterfeiting, we may identify a second best solution. This is to allow firms whose products are the subject of counterfeiting to enforce rights privately. Such firms would have the right to seize counterfeit goods and sell them on the market (presumably after removing the counterfeit trademark). It can be shown that this policy will not lead to optimal enforcement against counterfeiting, but it is preferable to no or to minimal public enforcement (Higgins and Rubin 1986). Some Western movie companies (including MGM, Warner, Sony and Paramount), have been training and financing full-time, private anti-piracy investigators for enforcement in Hungary. We would want to be sure, however, that such private enforcement was subject to ultimate control by the state, perhaps by allowing an appeal by the target firm.

Beyond this, governments can facilitate other investments in the creation of valuable brand names. Advertising is one prominent method of such investment. Government-owned radio and TV channels (if they cannot feasibly be privatized) should allow advertising. In Russia, as of

1993, 'the three television stations are government owned and run very limited advertising' (Tourevski and Morgan 1993, 105). However, more recently the amount of advertising on Russian TV has increased (Kranz 1994). As a result, many American brand names (Coca Cola, Procter & Gamble, Mars) are becoming well known in Russia. There is a private TV channel in the Czech Republic that sells substantial amounts of advertising (Durcanin 1995).

The Moscow and St Petersburg city governments have passed laws requiring one half of the words on all signs to be in Russian (Cyrillic) script, and that the Russian words must be twice as large as the others (Levine 1993). Such a law is harmful for several reasons. First, it increases the costs of advertising by requiring reconstruction of many signs. Second, it reduces the value of brand names, since companies would have chosen to advertise in whatever way would be most informative to consumers and mandated changes in advertising will therefore provide less information. Finally, by indicating to potential advertisers that they are willing arbitrarily and capriciously to destroy part of the value of past advertising, the government is reducing incentives for future investments in brand names.

In enforcing laws against deception, authorities should be careful not to over-regulate and deter the provision of valuable information (Rubin 1991). Provisions of the various laws regarding deception are sufficiently open-ended so that excess regulation is quite possible. It is particularly important to note that advertising is most likely to appear deceptive in a market that is not in equilibrium. Advertising in this context can be a powerful force for moving markets closer to equilibrium if it is allowed to do so.

In the post-communist economies, all markets may currently be out of equilibrium, and may remain so for some time. Moreover, consumers are likely to have relatively little experience or sophistication in dealing with advertising. Thus in the short run, much advertising might appear deceptive. However, excess regulation will reduce the rate of convergence of markets towards equilibrium, and increase the time it takes for consumers to learn how effectively to deal with advertising. Thus over-regulation is particularly likely and particularly costly in these economies.

Governments should keep in mind that an important incentive for the provision of quality is the higher price a firm can command for higher quality. At times (and particularly until markets have adjusted), those firms providing high quality will earn high profits. These profits will serve as a signal to other potential entrants that the provision of quality is worthwhile. However, authorities must be very careful not to reduce these incentives, for example by regulating (perhaps in the name of antitrust laws) prices charged. As entry occurs prices will naturally fall, but there must be rewards (perhaps very high rewards) for entrepreneurs who first learn the techniques valuable in a market economy.

BILATERAL MECHANISMS

There is relatively little government can do to facilitate bilateral agreements. Self-enforcing agreements, for example, do not need government assistance.

There is, however, substantial danger that improper and excessive use of antitrust policy could hinder the creation of bilateral arrangements. This fear is not based on pure speculation. In the USA improper antitrust policy has greatly hindered the creation of valuable vertical relationships between manufacturers and retailers (Posner 1981; Easterbrook 1984). Any contract between a manufacturer and a retailer should be strictly enforced by whatever enforcement mechanism is specified. The antitrust laws in all countries are sufficiently open-ended so that wealth-reducing over-regulation is at least possible.

Many of these antitrust laws apply only to firms with 'dominant' positions, commonly defined as market shares of 30 per cent or more. However, market shares are difficult to measure without sophisticated methods of defining markets. In US antitrust enforcement, market definition is often the most difficult and contested part of an enforcement action. Thus excessive enforcement is possible if decision-makers define markets too narrowly, as is likely and as has traditionally been true of US antitrust authorities. Aslund (1995, 153) indicates that markets have been narrowly defined in Russia. The Hungarian and CFR laws make it easier for a firm to be defined as a 'dominant' firm than is true in Poland and Russia, although any of the laws could be interpreted as excessively enforcing rules penalizing dominance.

One method of establishing credible commitments for bilateral relationships is the use of hostages. These require reciprocal dealing between firms; the antitrust laws have sometimes penalized this sort of behaviour. The Russian antitrust law forbids, 'imposing on the other party contractual terms that are disadvantageous to him or which are irrelevant to the subject-matter of the contract'. Other countries also forbid such practices. This can be interpreted as forbidding reciprocal transactions and the use of hostages. Again there should be no such restriction. All reciprocal transactions between firms should be legal.

It does not appear at this time that the antitrust laws are being abused. Many businessmen and attorneys indicate that there is a potential for abuse, but there does not seem to be a record of such behaviour. The Czech antitrust agency is located outside Prague, perhaps to weaken the agency and so minimize the danger of excessive enforcement. Similarly, the Polish antitrust agency is in Krakow, not Warsaw. Aslund (1995) indicates that in the past Russian anti-monopoly policy was excessively stringent, but that since 1994 it has been reformed and is likely less harmful.

MULTILATERAL ARRANGEMENTS

Governments have the greatest ability to be helpful with respect to multilateral enforcement mechanisms. Assistance can be provided to enable parties to benefit from such methods of enforcement by agreeing to enforce the decisions of arbitrators. Moreover, if properly done, governments can use the results of multilateral processes to generate efficient law. As of 1993, Poland was the only country studied that would enforce private arbitration agreements between domestic firms.

There are incentives for parties to contracts to choose efficient arbitrators in their agreements. Thus a decision by the courts or a statutory announcement that the courts will honour and enforce arbitration agreements may be the single most powerful method available for achieving efficient short-run decisions and also for generating efficient long-run precedents. (For reasons discussed below, the law may want to announce that it will enforce arbitration agreements only if there is a written opinion from the arbitrator in addition to a decision.)

As with other mechanisms, there is a danger of misuse of antitrust law with respect to trade associations. In particular, it will sometimes be necessary to exclude some firms from the association in order to maintain quality. However, incorrect antitrust law can interpret such exclusion as being an anti-competitive boycott. Moreover, the Russian antitrust law requires that all such associations be approved by the antitrust authorities. This could make the formation of such organizations more difficult. Correct interpretation will be difficult, as such associations can indeed be used for anti-competitive exclusion.

8. Creation of Efficient Rules

The private mechanisms discussed here can be used as the basis for an efficient body of law. I first discuss the mechanisms for such law creation. I then discuss some of the benefits of private law creation. In particular, private law may have some advantages over public law.

MECHANISMS

One advantage of the set of institutions proposed here (and in particular of the multilateral institutions) is that these may actually lead to the evolution of efficient rules. There are mechanisms that might lead a formal legal system to evolve efficient rules, but the power of these mechanisms is limited (Rubin 1977; Landes and Posner 1979). Competing jurisdictions and competition between judges may be the most efficient method of achieving efficient rules quickly. Indeed the common law courts adopted the relatively efficient rules of the private Law Merchant in order to obtain the legal business (and associated fees) of merchants. For such competition to be effective, parties must be able to choose *ex ante* which court will hear their dispute because this will give courts incentives to seek efficient solutions to get more business. In the system in Russia, although there are three separate court systems, they do not seem to compete *ex ante* for business, and parties do not seem able *ex ante* to choose the court that will hear their dispute.

When parties negotiate contracts in good faith (that is, without plans to breach), they will consider methods of enforcement. Generally speaking, breach of a contract will occur only in the event of unanticipated events, so parties cannot know *ex ante* the nature of a breach or the desired remedies. Therefore, the interest of parties *ex ante* is to choose those arbitrators who will maximize the *ex post* joint wealth of the parties – that is, who will choose efficient rules for enforcement. If these arbitrators then establish rules through announcing the reasons for their decisions, the rules will tend to be efficient. If they are not, then disputants in the future will choose different arbitrators. There will be strong pressures for arbitrators who use efficient rules.

Landes and Posner (1979) argue that there is sometimes an inadequate incentive for arbitration to produce rules (as opposed to decisions) because the creation of rules does not benefit the parties who pay for dispute settlement. The rule is a public good whose private value may be less than the cost to the disputants. This has been questioned on factual grounds by Benson (1990), who points out that the Law Merchant did produce rules that were later adopted into the common law. Moreover, Benson suggests that if parties contract in advance with arbitrators, then arbitrators have an incentive to make the rules they will use in the event of a dispute clear in order to facilitate settlement and reduce the number of cases actually arbitrated.

Landes and Posner (1979) agree that there are circumstances in which rules will be created. If the arbitration is performed for an association, then rule creation is feasible because the association can collect dues and use these to pay for rules. The Law Merchant evolved at least in part in connection with trade fairs (one example is the Champagne Fairs), and therefore there was a possibility of creating efficient rules because all participants in the Fairs would have been willing to pay a share for such rule creation and the organizers could have charged a premium to support this outcome (Milgrom *et al.* 1990). As suggested above, a possible method to generate rules would be for the state to agree to enforce arbitration agreements only if the arbitrator agrees to write an opinion.

For private associations, dues could be used to supplement fees paid by disputants and therefore pay for rule creation and promulgation. The rules would benefit all members of the association, not merely those with a dispute at issue, and so members would be willing to pay dues to obtain such rules. Associations depend on members for dues. Firms would be more likely to join associations if the associations credibly promised them efficient rules. Customary rules used in an industry are a likely source of efficient precedents (Epstein 1992; Cooter 1994), and the mechanisms identified here are useful for generation of formal records of such customs. Bernstein (1995) is undertaking a major study of such private associations, and her results should be directly relevant for the issues raised here.

CHARACTERISTICS OF PRIVATE LAW

There will be other advantages of private law. Although it is not possible to describe the details of efficient contract law for each country at each point in time, some broad properties of such law can be described. This is particularly true since American contract law is in some respects inefficient, and it is possible to identify the areas of inefficiency.

In particular, law can err by refusing to enforce voluntarily agreed upon contract terms. In the USA and elsewhere today, courts brand certain types of contract as being 'against public policy'. Such contracts may be considered 'unconscionable'. The courts claim that the parties had 'unequal bargaining power' or that the relevant contracts were 'contracts of adhesion'. Such rulings are particularly common in contracts between individuals and business firms, but sometimes apply to other contracts as well. In these cases, courts will refuse to enforce the contracts.

None of these doctrines is desirable. In all cases, they make the parties to transactions worse off. All of these doctrines have been imposed by courts on parties who have signed contracts with provisions that, *ex post* (after breach, or after an accident) one of the parties has regretted. If there is private enforcement of contracts, then courts will not adopt any such inefficient provisions; courts will enforce contracts as written. Thus private enforcement will lead to a more efficient contract law than would public enforcement, if public enforcement follows the US example.

Of course, there are some contracts that are inefficient. However, these are generally inefficient with respect to third parties. Two examples are contracts to fix prices and contracts to commit a crime. These sorts of agreement can be eliminated by other branches of law: the antitrust laws[22] and criminal laws Moreover, since such contracts are illegal, the parties would want to keep them secret, and thus would not rely on the sort of private mechanisms discussed here, even if these mechanisms could lead to enforcement. Thus with respect to those contracts that are economically efficient and socially desirable, it is likely that there would be some advantages to private enforcement relative to public enforcement. Indeed the best of all worlds might be private determination of liability (as by arbitrators or trade associations) with public enforcement of the private decrees.

Two-party contracts might be inefficient if one party to the contract is incompetent. This might apply to contracts with children or with the mentally incompetent on one side. Contracts will also be inefficient if there is fraud or duress, where duress is defined as involving force, not 'unequal bargaining power' (Posner 1992, 114–17) or 'unconscionability' (Epstein 1976). The medieval Law Merchant, a voluntary body of contract law, would invalidate a contract based on, 'fraud, duress, or other abuses of the will or knowledge of either party' (Benson 1989, 649). Thus private law should be able to handle these problems of inefficient contract formation.

9. Implications

This work provides suggestions for behaviour for governments, arbitrators, private trade associations, private attorneys and businesses in the post-communist economies. I consider each.

Before discussing particular policies, however, a word about Russia is needed. The policy discussion assumes that those in authority desire to develop a market economy and to maximize social wealth, perhaps subject to normal political constraints. This may not be true in Russia. If it is not, then more fundamental change, going beyond the analysis in this work (or beyond the normal suggestions of economists in policy matters) is needed. The nature of the changes was discussed in Chapter 6. Specifically, government must honour its own commitments and enforce promises made by others. If the Russian government can credibly promise to do so, then development is possible. If not, then the country may remain trapped in a low level, crime-ridden equilibrium. Here I deal with policies useful for economies where authorities do want a more efficient market economy. The examples of Poland, Hungary and the Czech Republic indicate that it is possible to succeed in creating institutions to emerge from the wreckage created by communism.

Public choice economists treat government policy as the product of self-interested behaviour by politicians and interest groups. From an extreme public choice viewpoint, policy recommendations may not be useful because existing policies are the product of the set of politically effective pressures that exists in a society at a point in time. There are two points to make with respect to the issues analysed here.

First, it may be possible to use existing interest group pressures to develop more efficient policies. In their discussion of privatization, Boycko *et al.* (1994) explicitly discuss the use of public choice theory in designing privatization schemes that can benefit from the set of interests in place. Since the authors of this article were also instrumental in designing the relatively successful Russian privatization scheme, we must judge this effort as being useful.

Second, this work deals with private law issues, such as contract law. While it is sometimes possible for special interest groups to use private law mechanisms for rent-seeking (Rubin and Bailey 1994) the circumstances under which this is possible are limited. In particular, Rubin and Bailey show that lawyers can sometimes change the law in ways to benefit themselves. However, this possibility is not likely in Russia. First, there are not enough lawyers, and they are not sufficiently powerful. Second, given the small number of lawyers and the underdeveloped state of the legal system, lawyers could probably make more money now by developing more efficient law. Creation of inefficient law for rent-seeking only pays when there is an excessively large number of lawyers in an economy.

However, there are some examples of inefficient Russian law benefiting particular interest groups. Many of the identified inefficiencies are with respect to managers of firms using stock market manipulations of various sorts to disempower investors, discussed at length earlier. While the long-term interests of managers may be in a more open and efficient system of corporate control, the short-term interest of existing managers is in maintaining their position. Moreover, existing managers may not be the best candidates in a market economy, since many of them rose to their positions under the previous regime, so they may fear the loss of their jobs if capital markets begin to work better. Problems of managerial opportunism and shirking are substantial in the USA and other developed economies (for example, Rubin 1990, Chapter 5), and it will be difficult to solve them in Russia. The Czech Republic solved these problems by rapid privatization, so that managers did not have time to organize and delay the process. It is too late for this solution in Russia.

For those parts of the law where such pressures are less strong or do not exist, such as the domain of classical contract law, then there are benefits from more efficient law and few, if any, who would lose. How, then, can we explain the general inefficiency of Russian law? One simple possibility is ignorance: no one in power in Russia may understand the nature of efficient law and its benefits. A second possibility is time: it may simply take more time for efficient law to come into existence than has been available since the collapse of communism. Third, one point emphasized throughout this work is uncertainty: it may not pay for anyone to invest in creating efficient law because of the uncertain pay-off. Since this work has attempted to set forth policies that will enable law to become more efficient more quickly, it may serve to help solve these problems. It is in this spirit that I offer the following explicit policy suggestions.

Governments

Government policy was discussed at length in Chapter 7. Briefly, for governments the major implication is that enforcement of private agreements to arbitrate disputes between domestic firms, as well as between domestic and foreign firms, is useful and desirable. This simple policy would be the most powerful device for quickly adapting the dispute resolution system for a market economy. Governments might want to consider paying a small subsidy to arbitrators if they agree to write opinions, but this is of secondary importance. If arbitrators begin adopting a set of rules and precedents, then governments should consider these in revisions of commercial codes. Governments may also want to make provisions for a common law-type process for the court system during times between revisions of codes.

Other government policies are mainly negative in nature. Governments should refrain from excessive enforcement of antitrust laws, including regulation of vertical relationships, and laws against deception. Western economies established market institutions and developed large economies before such inefficient law enforcement became fashionable, and if new economies unduly burden themselves with such costly policies, growth might be retarded or even precluded. In the case of Russia, a strengthening of the central government is necessary so that it will be possible for government itself credibly to commit to policies facilitating growth. Government should also begin to honour its own agreements so that promises to enforce the commitments of others will be credible.

Arbitrators

If a government will enforce arbitration decrees, then arbitrators can play a major role in the system. The government should pay for some arbitration association to announce that it will establish precedents and decide cases based on these precedents. If this policy is successful and if parties begin using this association, then the association might begin to charge *ex ante* for being named in contracts as the arbitrator of choice. Law firms might find the provision of such arbitration a valuable specialty.

Trade Associations

Private trade associations can begin to play an informational role. Such associations can keep records of behaviour of members of the industry and make this information available to potential transactors. This can be done for a fee paid by those seeking the information. Alternatively, the trade association can charge members for listing. Any firm not listed would then signal to potential partners that it was unwilling to be rated by the association. Trade associations can also establish formal arbitration procedures with enforcement through information and reputation mechanisms. Organizations such as Better Business Bureaus can perform a similar function for businesses (perhaps retail businesses) in a geographic location.

Attorneys

Private attorneys advising firms can make use of information regarding reputations as it becomes generated. Attorneys can also include arbitration clauses in contracts for their clients. Indeed attorneys could now include clauses indicating that arbitration will be used if arbitration decrees should become enforceable in the future. If certain arbitration associations begin to generate precedents, and if these seem useful and efficient, attorneys can name these associations in contracts.

Businesses

Businesses can make use of all the information generated by the processes mentioned above. In addition, certain behaviours of businesses in post-communist economies may be remnants of their past, and are now counterproductive. First, businesses should avoid excessive secrecy. The best way to guarantee performance is to establish a reputation for fair and honest dealing. Creation of reputations is by definition an activity requiring information-sharing, and excessive secrecy can hinder or stop this activity. Second, businesses should become more accommodating in their bargaining strategies. For agreements to be self-enforcing, both parties must value the expected future benefits of continuing the sequence of transacting at more than the one-time benefits of cheating. Businesses with long time horizons should realize this and allow trading partners to make a reasonable return on the stream of transactions.

While the transition from a planned to a market economy and the elimination of the harms caused by communism will take a long time, adoption of the policies suggested here can speed up the process and also increase wealth and thus consumer welfare during the transition period.

Notes

1. I deal specifically with Hungary, Poland, the Czech Republic and especially with Russia, countries I have visited. However, I believe the general principles discussed will be more widely applicable.
2. Some exceptions are IMF (1991), Niskanen (1991), Pittman (1992), Gray and Associates (1993), Greif and Kandel (1995) and Pistor (1995).
3. For a discussion of efficient contract law, see Posner (1992, Chapter 4).
4. 'Probably some combination of private adjudication with ultimate state authority to back up its decisions is the most that a rapidly emerging free-market system can hope for' (Manne 1991, 213). Shavell (1995) agrees that it is efficient to enforce arbitration agreements if the parties voluntarily agree to such agreements *ex ante*.
5. Since I write from a libertarian perspective, a claim that a government has insufficient power is not one I make lightly. However, libertarianism is not anarchism, and libertarians believe that government does have some worthwhile functions and requires sufficient power to undertake these functions. Law enforcement is generally accepted as one such function.
6. It has been suggested at a seminar that a country could import judges and lawyers to operate such a code. This might solve some of the problems, but does not seem a practical alternative. Moreover, language problems would persist.
7. Except for Louisiana.
8. I met with many such attorneys in several countries. Almost all of them were associated with major American law firms, and many who were not seemed able to engage in significant amounts of consulting for foreign businesses. Others were in prestigious positions with important government ministries.
9. A 'quasi-rent' is a return on a fixed investment. Once a fixed investment is made, its return can be expropriated. If it were known in advance that the quasi-rent would be expropriated, then the initial investment would never have been made.
10. Landa (1981). For an interesting formal model of an ethnically based trading network involving the Maghribi, with enforcement mechanisms, see Avner Greif (1993). The Maghribi were 11th century Jewish traders in the Mediterranean.
11. The working out of the effects of this insight on vertical integration was in part due to Klein *et al.* (1978); see also Williamson (1985) and Rubin (1990).
12. Discussed in Greif and Kandel (1995).
13. This information is from Yakovlev (1994). Yakovlev is the Chairman of the Supreme Arbitration Court.
14. There are some other likely difficulties with this law which are important, although not directly relevant to the issues in this paper. The law adopts many of the errors in contemporary American contract law. Article 333 limits contractual damages to an amount which is not, 'clearly incommensurate to the consequences of the violation', equivalent to common law courts' (mistaken) unwillingness to enforce contractually specified damages viewed as 'punitive'. Article 426 allows dissolution of 'contracts of adhesion'. In addition, Article 10 states: 'The use by commercial organizations of civil rights for the purpose of limiting competition, and also abuse by them of their dominant position in the market, shall not be

permitted'. This is an extremely open-ended antitrust law, with great potential for abuse.

15. For example, Viechtbauer (1993), p. 363: 'In addition, the current Russian judicial system, because of deficiencies in staffing, regulation, and infrastructure, cannot reasonably be expected to handle any commercial disputes, let alone international trade cases'.

16. These examples are based on various stories in the *Moscow Times* from 25–29 May 1993.

17. Elf is 50 per cent owned by the French government, so that investment decisions might be made for political reasons. Normally, major stockholders would be expected to monitor such activity, but Elf's, 'management has been making its own decisions for many years – including its journey to the East – with little supervision by the state'.

18. Similar problems may exist in China (see Smith and Brauchli 1995).

19. This book is a very interesting but depressing study of the role of crime in Russia today, with implications well beyond the scope of this work. The theme of the book is that there are close links between government, business and criminals.

20. Soros believes that the most fundamental struggle in Russia is between energy producers and energy users. The former can sell on world markets, and are therefore in favour of reform and open markets. The latter include the large, inefficient industrial and military sector. Unfortunately, Soros believes the latter group is winning.

21. Tainter (1988) is a fascinating study of collapse, and many of the conditions discussed are observed in the former Soviet Union in areas not relevant to the concerns of this paper. One weakness of the book is its prediction that: 'Collapse today is neither an option nor an immediate threat'. Moreover, although writing in 1988, Tainter considered and rejected only the possibility of the collapse of Western civilization; the collapse of the Soviet Union was not contemplated.

22. Although I have discussed inappropriate use of these laws, outlawing of explicit price-fixing agreements is probably within the proper scope of the antitrust laws. Of course, it may be difficult to confine regulators to the appropriate use of these laws.

Bibliography

Akerlof, George A. (1970), 'The market for lemons: qualitative uncertainty and the market mechanism', *Quarterly Journal of Economics*, **84**, 488.

Aslund, Anders (1992), *Post-Communist Economic Revolutions: How Big a Bang?*, Washington: The Center for Strategic and International Studies.

Aslund, Anders (1994), 'Russia's success story', *Foreign Affairs*, September/October, 58–71.

Aslund, Anders (1995), *How Russia Became a Market Economy*, Washington: Brookings Institution.

Banerjee, Neela (1995a), 'Russian oil company tries a stock split in the Soviet style: Komineft didn't tell holders, many of whom didn't get any of the new shares', *Wall Street Journal*, 15 February, p. A14.

Banerjee, Neela (1995b), 'Russian securities trading, a business with a past, bets future on regulation', *Wall Street Journal*, 8 February, p. A11.

Banerjee, Neela and Gabriela Teodorescu (1995), 'Russians become homey with mortgages: pent-up housing demand lends hand to concept', *Wall Street Journal*, 28 September, p. A10.

Benson, Bruce L. (1989), 'The spontaneous evolution of commercial law', *Southern Economic Journal*, **55**, 644–61.

Benson, Bruce L. (1990), *The Enterprise of Law*, San Francisco: Pacific Research Institute.

Benson, Bruce L. (1992), 'Customary law as social contract: international commercial law', *Constitutional Political Economy*, **3**, 1–27.

Berman, Harold J. (1983), *Law and Revolution: The Formation of the Western Legal Tradition*, Cambridge: Harvard University Press.

Bernstein, Lisa (1992), 'Opting out of the legal system: extralegal contractual relations in the diamond industry', *Journal of Legal Studies*, **21**, 115–59.

Bernstein, Lisa (1995), 'Project summary: the newest law merchant: private commercial law in the United States', paper presented at the American Law and Economics Association Meeting, Berkeley.

Black, Bernard S., Reinier H. Kraakman and Jonathan Hay (1995), 'Corporate law from scratch', Columbia University School of Law, Center for Law and Economic Studies, Working Paper, #104, forthcoming in Cheryl Gray, Andrzej Rapaczynski and Roman Frydman (eds), *Corporate Governance in Eastern Europe*, World Bank, in press.

Boettke, Peter J. (1995), 'Credibility, commitment, and Soviet economic reform', in E. Lazear (ed.), *Economic Transition in Eastern Europe and Russia: Realities of Reform*, Stanford, California: Hoover Institution Press.

Boycko, Maxim, Andrei Shleifer and Robert W. Vishny (1994), 'Voucher privatization', *Journal of Financial Economics*, vol. 35, 249–266.

Branegan, Jay (1994), 'White knights need not apply', *Time*, 31 October.

Burandt, Gary (1992), *Moscow Meets Madison Avenue: The Adventures of the First Adman in the USSR*, New York: HarperBusiness.

Buyevich, Alexander J. and Sergey N. Zhukov (1992), 'Dispute resolution in Russia', *Law of the Newly Independent States: The Bottom Line*.

Clague, Christopher, Philip Keefer, Steven Kanck and Mancur Olson (1995), 'Contract Intensive Money: Contract Enforcement, Property Rights, and Economic Performance', University of Maryland.

Coase, Ronald H. (1937), 'The nature of the firm', *Economica*, 386, reprinted in Coase, *The Firm, the Market and the Law*, Chicago: University of Chicago Press, 1988, pp. 33–55.

Coase, Ronald H. (1960), 'The Problem of Social Cost', *Journal of Law and Economics*.

Cooter, Robert D. (1994), 'Structural adjudication and the new Law Merchant: a model of decentralized law', *International Review of Law and Economics*, **14**.

Cowley, Andrew (1995), 'Russia's emerging market', *The Economist*, 8 April.

Craik, Euan (1995), 'Investors rate legal mess as key obstacle', *Moscow Times*, 1 April, p. 1.

Dubik, Mikhail (1994a), 'Of debts and decrees', *Business Central Europe*, November, p. 54.

Dubik, Mikhail (1994b), 'Top firms sign investors bill of rights', *Moscow Times*, 6 October.

Dunkin, Amy (1995), 'After the fire in emerging markets', *Business Week*, 23 January.

Durcanin, Cynthia (1995), 'Whips, chains, car crashes and bingo', *Business Week* (international edition), 20 February.

Easterbrook, Frank H. (1984), 'Vertical arrangements and the rule of reason', *Antitrust Law Journal*, **53**, 135.

Economist (1995a), 'Boris the broker evolves: Russia's primitive stockmarket is at last becoming more sophisticated', 8 July, 69–70.

Economist (1995b), 'Russian law: groping ahead', 2 September, pp. 42–8.

Epstein, Richard A. (1975), 'Unconscionability: a critical reappraisal', *Journal of Law and Economics*, **18**, 292–316.

Epstein, Richard A. (1992), 'The path to the *T.J. Hooper*: the theory and history of custom in the law of tort', *Journal of Legal Studies*, **21**, 1–39.

Erlanger, Steven (1994), 'Russia's new dictatorship of crime', *New York Times*, 15 May.

Erlanger, Steven (1995), 'In Russia, official corruption is worse than organized crime', *New York Times*, 3 July.

Filipov, David (1994), 'Civil code promises to untie red tape', *Moscow Times*, 28 July, p. 3.

Fogel, Marya (1995a), 'Foreigners learn to cope – sort of – with Russia's ever-mutating laws', *Wall Street Journal*, 7 July, p. A6.

Fogel, Marya (1995b), 'Russia expands a tax on payrolls, angering many foreign businesses', *Wall Street Journal*, 5 April, p. A9.

Fogel, Marya and Anne Reifenberg (1995), 'Russia may face an oil rush in reverse: tax laws, export quotas drive western firms away', *Wall Street Journal*, 14 February, p. A19.

Frye, Timothy (1995), 'Contracting in the shadow of the state: private arbitration courts in Russia', prepared for presentation for the John M. Olin Seminar Series, 'The Rule of Law and Economic Reform in Russia', Harvard University.

Galuszka, Peter (1994), 'Only the stubborn strike it rich in Russia', *Business Week* (international edition), 12 September.

Galuszka, Peter and Susan Chandler (1995), 'Russia: a plague of disjointed ventures', *Business Week* (international edition), 1 May.

Galuszka, Peter and Sandra Dallas (1995), 'And you think you've got tax problems', *Business Week*, 29 May.

Galuszka, Peter and Patricia Kranz (1995), 'Look who's making a revolution: shareholders', *Business Week*, 20 February.

Galuszka, Peter, Patricia Kranz and Stanley Reed (1994), 'Russia's new capitalism: it's still chaotic, but private companies are forging a vital economy', *Business Week*, 10 October.

Goldberg, Paul (1992), 'Economic reform and product quality improvement efforts in the Soviet Union', *Soviet Studies*, **44**, 113–22.

Goldman, Marshall I. (1994), *Lost Opportunity: Why Economic Reforms in Russia have not worked*, New York: W.W. Norton.

Gordon, Michael R. (1995), 'Cautiously pessimistic investor eyes Russia', *The New York Times*, 22 December.

Gray, Cheryl W. and Associates (1993), *Evolving Legal Frameworks for Private Sector Development in Central and Eastern Europe*, World Bank Discussion Paper 209, July.

Greif, Avner (1993), 'Contract enforceability and economic institutions in early trade: the Maghribi traders coalition', *American Economic Review*, **83**, 525–44.

Greif, Avner (1994), 'Cultural beliefs and the organization of society: a historical and theoretical reflection on collectivist and individualist societies', *Journal of Political Economy*, **102**, 912–50.

Greif, Avner and Eugene Kandel (1995), 'Contract enforcement institutions: historical perspective and current status in Russia', in E. Lazear (ed.), *Economic Transition in Eastern Europe and Russia: Realities of Reform*, Stanford, California: Hoover Institution Press.

Gurkov, Igor and Gary Asselbergs (1995), 'Ownership and control in Russian privatised companies: evidence from a survey', *Communist Economies & Economic Transformation*, **7**, 195–211.

Halligan, Liam and Pavel Teplukin (1995), 'Investment disincentives in Russia', preliminary draft, mimeo.

Handelman, Stephen (1995), *Comrade Criminal: Russia's New Mafia*, New Haven: Yale University Press.

Hayek, Friedrich A. (1973), *Law, Legislation and Liberty; Volume 1: Rules and Order*, Chicago: University of Chicago Press.

Higgins, Richard S. and Paul H. Rubin (1986), 'Counterfeit goods', *Journal of Law and Economics*, **29**, 211–30.

Hill, Ivan (ed.) (1976), *The Ethical Basis of Economic Freedom*, Chapel Hill, North Carolina: American Viewpoint.

Imse, Ann (1993), 'American know-how and Russian oil', *The New York Times Magazine*, 7 March.

International Monetary Fund (IMF), The World Bank, Organization for Economic Cooperation and Development, and European Bank for Reconstruction and Development (1991), *A Study of the Soviet Economy*, Washington: IMF *et al.*

Intriligator, Michael D. (1994), 'Privatization in Russia has led to criminalization', *The Australian Economic Review*, **4**, 4–14.

Johnson, Simon and Heidi Kroll (1991), 'Managerial strategies for spontaneous privatization', *Soviet Economy*, **7**, 281–316.

Jones, Anthony (1992), 'Issues in state and private sector relations in the Soviet Economy', in Bruno Dallago, Gianmaria Ajani and Bruno Grancelli (eds), *Privatization and Entrepreneurship in Post-Socialist Countries: Economy, Law and Society*, New York: St Martin's Press, 69–88.

Jones, Anthony and William Moskoff (1991), *Ko-ops: The Rebirth of Entrepreneurship in the Soviet Union*, Bloomington: Indiana University Press.

Klein, Benjamin (1992), 'Contracts and incentives: the role of contact terms in assuring performance', in Lars Werin and Hans Wijkander (eds), *Contract Economics*, Cambridge, MA: Blackwell, 149–72.

Klein, Benjamin, Robert Crawford, and Armen Alchian (1978), 'Vertical integration, appropriable rents, and the competitive contracting process', *Journal of Law and Economics*, **21**, 297.

Klein, Benjamin and Keith B. Leffler (1981), 'The role of market forces in assuring contractual performance', *Journal of Political Economy*, **89**, 615.

Kornai, Janos (1992), 'The postsocialist transition and the state: reflections in the light of Hungarian fiscal problems', *American Economic Review*, **82**, 1–21.

Kranz, Patricia (1994), 'In Moscow, the attack of the killer brands', *Business Week*, 10 January.

Kranz, Patricia (1995a), 'Russia's really hostile takeovers', *Business Week*, 14 August.

Kranz, Patricia (1995b), 'Russia isn't Siberia for investors anymore', *Business Week* (international edition), 17 April.

Kranz, Patricia and Karen Lowry Miller (1994), 'Lost in the translations', *Business Week*, 3 October.

Kroll, Heidi (1987), 'Breach of contract in the Soviet economy', *Journal of Legal Studies*, **16**, 119–48.

Kvint, Vladimir (1993), *The Barefoot Shoemaker: Capitalizing on the New Russia*, New York: Arcade Publishing.

Landa, Janet T. (1981), 'A theory of the ethnically homogeneous middleman group: an institutional alternative to contract law', *Journal of Legal Studies*, **10**, 349–62.

Landes, William M. and Richard A. Posner (1979), 'Adjudication as a private good', *Journal of Legal Studies*, **8**, 235–84.

Langer, Robert and Alexander Buyevitch (1995), 'Russia's courts take courage', *Moscow Times*, 18 July, p. 17.

Leijonhufvud, Axel (1993), 'Problems of socialist transition: Kazakhstan 1991', in Laszlo Samogyi (ed.), *The Political Economy of the Transition Process in Eastern Europe*, Aldershot: Edward Elgar, pp. 289–311.

Leitzel, Jim, Clifford Gaddy and Michael Alexeev (1995), 'Mafiosi and Matrioshki: organized crime and Russian reform', *Brookings Review*, 26–29.

Leoni, Bruno (1961; 1991 edition), *Freedom and the Law*, Indianapolis: Liberty Fund.

Levine, Joanne (1993), 'Cyrill rights', *Business Central Europe*, May, p. 32.

Levy, Marcia (1995), 'A look back at '94: progress, promise', *Moscow Times*, 17 January, p. 17.

Liesman, Steve (1995a), 'Russian shipping firm doubles number of shares without consulting investors', *Wall Street Journal*, 4 April, p. A16.

Liesman, Steve (1995b), 'High noon at Russia's annual meetings: directors resent intrusions by "outside" shareholders', *Wall Street Journal*, 21 April, p. A7.

Liesman, Steve (1995c), 'A big buildup: despite long odds, construction work is booming in Moscow: shaky financing and a lack of property laws make office projects risky', *Wall Street Journal*, 28 December.

Liesman, Steve (1995d), 'For US investors, Russia rates caution: enthusiasm fades as Moscow's market fizzles', *Wall Street Journal*, 23 October.

Liesman, Steve and Martin du Bois (1995), 'Russia's "mineral wealth": a dubious buried treasure: investors are deterred by remote and exaggerated reserves, as well as vague laws', *Wall Street Journal*, 22 February, p. A17.

Los, Maria (1992), 'From underground to legitimacy: the normative dilemmas of post-communist marketization', in Bruno Dallago, Gianmaria Ajani and Bruno Grancelli (eds), *Privatization and Entrepreneurship in Post-Socialist Countries: Economy. Law and Society*, New York: St Martin's Press, 111–42.

Manne, Henry (1991), 'Perestroika and the limits of knowledge', *Cato Journal*, **11**, 207–14.

Mauro, Paolo (1995), 'Corruption and growth', *Quarterly Journal of Economics*, **90**, (3), August, 681–712.

Mileusnic, Natasha (1995a), 'New law threatens foreign tax breaks', *Moscow Times*, 28 March.

Mileusnic, Natasha (1995b), 'Securities bill "ruined" by Duma', *Moscow Times*, 29 March.

Milgrom, Paul R., Douglass C. North and Barry W. Weingast (1990), 'The role of institutions in the revival of trade: the law merchant, private judges, and the Champagne Fairs', *Economics and Politics*, **2**, 1–23.

Miller, Karen Lowry, Frank J. Comes and Peggy Simpson (1995), 'Poland: rising star of Europe', *Business Week*, 4 December.

Miller, Karen Lowry, Peggy Simpson and Tim Smart (1994), 'Europe: The Push East', *Business Week*, 7 November.

Moore, Stephen D. (1993), 'Sweden's Ikea forges into Eastern Europe', *Wall Street Journal*, 28 June, p. B6E.

Moscow Times (1995), 'Komineft to annul secret issue', 1 March, p. 14.

Muris, Timothy J. (1981), 'Opportunistic behavior and the law of contracts', *Minnesota Law Review*, **65**, 527.

Murrell, Peter (1991), 'Conservative political philosophy and the strategy of economic transition', IRIS Working Paper No. 7, University of Maryland.

Niskanen, William (1991), 'The soft infrastructure of a market economy', *Cato Journal*, **11**, 233–8.

North, Douglass (1991), 'Institutions, ideology and economic performance', *Cato Journal*, **11**, 477–88.

Osakwe, Christopher (1993), 'Modern Russian law of banking and security transactions: a biopsy of post-Soviet Russian commercial law', *Whittier Law Review*, **V** (14), 301–82.

Pennar, Karen, Peter Galuszka and Karen Lowry Miller (1994), 'Frontier economies: enter if you dare', *Business Week*, 18 November.

Perlez, Jane (1993), 'Poland's new entrepreneurs push the economy ahead', *New York Times*, Sunday 20 June, p. F7.

Pistor, Katharina (1995), 'Supply and demand for contract enforcement in Russia: courts, arbitration, and private enforcement', Prepared for presentation for the John M. Olin Seminar Series, 'The Rule of Law and Economic Reform in Russia', Harvard University.

Pittman, Russell (1992), 'Some critical provisions in the antimonopoly laws of Central and Eastern Europe', *The International Lawyer*, **26**, 485–503.

Poe, Richard (1993), *How to Profit from the Coming Russian Boom: The Insider's Guide to Business Opportunities and Survival on the Frontiers of Capitalism*, New York: McGraw-Hill.

Posner, Richard A. (1981), 'The next step in the antitrust treatment of restricted distribution: per se legality', *University of Chicago Law Review*, **40**, 6.

Posner, Richard A. (1992), *Economic Analysis of Law*, Boston: Little, Brown and Co.

Rossant, Juliette (1994), 'In Moscow, it's location, location, location', *Business Week*, 25 July.

Rubin, Paul H. (1977), 'Why is the common law efficient?', *Journal of Legal Studies*, **6**, 51–63.

Rubin, Paul H. (1990), *Managing Business Transactions: Controlling the Costs of Coordinating, Communicating and Decision Making*, New York: Free Press.

Rubin, Paul H. (1991), 'Economics and the regulation of deception', *Cato Journal*, **11**, 667–90.

Rubin, Paul H. (1993), 'Private mechanisms for creation of efficient institutions for market economies', in Laszlo Samogyi (ed.), *The Political Economy of the Transition Process in Eastern Europe*, Aldershot: Edward Elgar, pp. 158–70.

Rubin, Paul H. and Martin Bailey (1994), 'The role of lawyers in changing the law', *Journal of Legal Studies*, June, 807–31.

Russian Federation (1994), *Civil Code of the Russian Federation, Studies on Russian Law*, London: the Vinogradoff Institute, Faculty of Laws, University College of London.

Sachs, Jeffrey D. (1995), 'Why corruption rules Russia', *The New York Times*, 29 November, p. A19.

Salpukas, Agis (1993), 'In an oil rush to the East, Elf plays pied piper', *The New York Times*, 27 June, p. F7.

Schmid, A. Allan (1992), 'Legal foundations of the market: implications for the formerly socialist countries of Eastern Europe and Africa', *Journal of Economic Issues*, **26**, 707–32.

Scully, Gerald W. (1992), *Constitutional Environments and Economic Growth*, Princeton: Princeton University Press.

Shavell, Steven (1995), 'Alternative dispute resolution: an economic analysis', *Journal of Legal Studies*, **24**, 1–28.

Shiller, Robert J., Maxim Boycko and Vladimir Korobov (1992), 'Hunting for *Homo Sovieticus*: situational versus attitudinal factors in economic behavior', *Brookings Papers on Economic Activity*, **1**, 127–94.

Shleifer, Andrei and Robert W. Vishny (1993), 'Corruption', *Quarterly Journal of Economics*, **108**, 599.

Siltchenkov, Dimitri (1993), 'A stranger in a strange land: practicing law after the breakup of the USSR', *Whittier Law Review*, **V** (14), 503–14.

Simpson, Peggy (1995), 'As Poland embraces the franchise – a master baker cooks up his own', *Business Week* (international edition), 26 June.

Smith, Craig and Marcus Brauchli (1995), 'The long march: to invest successfully in China, foreigners find patience crucial, *Wall Street Journal*, 23 February, p. 1.

Stanley, Alessandra (1995), 'To the business risks in Russia, add poisoning', *New York Times*, 9 August.

Tainter, Joseph A. (1988), *The Collapse of Complex Societies*, New York: Cambridge University Press.

Telser, Lester (1980), 'A theory of self enforcing agreements', *Journal of Business*, **53**, 27.

Thomas, Bill and Charles Sutherland (1992), *Red Tape: Adventure Capitalism in the New Russia*, New York: Dutton.

Tolkacheva, Julie (1995), 'Troika-Dialog JV sues first voucher', *Moscow Times*, 24 January, p. 13.

Topornin, Boris N. (1993), *The Legal Problems of Economic Reform in Russia*, Edinburgh: The David Hume Institute.

Tourevski, Mark and Eileen Morgan (1993), *Cutting the Red Tape: How Western Companies Can Profit in the New Russia*, New York: Free Press.

Toy, Stewart and Karen Lowry Miller (1995), 'An island breeze blows in Prague', *Business Week*, 11 December.

Uchitelle, Lewis (1992), 'The art of a Russian deal: ad-libbing contract law', *New York Times*, 17 January, p. 1.

Vasiliev, Dmitry (1995), 'We Russians can mind our own markets', *Wall Street Journal*, 7 July, p. A10.

Viechtbauer, Volker (1993), 'Arbitration in Russia', *Stanford Journal of International Law*, **V** (29), 355.

Vlasihin, Vasily A. (1993), 'Toward a rule of law and bill of rights for Russia', in Bruce L.R. Smith and Gennady M. Danilenko (eds), *Law and Democracy in the New Russia*, Washington: Brookings Institution.

Wegren, Stephen K. (1994), 'Building market institutions', *Communist and Post-Communist Studies*, **V** (27), 195–224.

Weingast, Barry (1995), 'The economic role of political institutions: market-preserving federalism and economic development', *Journal of Law, Economics and Organization*, **V** (11), April, 1–31.

Williamson, Oliver E. (1985), *The Economic Institutions of Capitalism*, New York: Free Press.

Winestock, Geoff (1995), 'Standoff in smuggler's paradise', *Business Week* (international edition), 25 September.

Wolf, Holger C. (1993), 'Endogenous legal booms', *Journal of Law, Economics, & Organization*, **9**, 181–7.

Yakovlev, Veniamin Fedorovich (1994), 'Interview', *Moscow Rossiyskaya Gazeta*, reprinted in *Federal Broadcast Information Service-USSR*, p. -077, 19 July.

Zhurek, Stephan (1993), 'Commodity exchanges in Russia: success or failure', *Radio Liberty Research Report*, **2**, 41–4.

Index